'To make progress in life requires good and solid decisions – this book s̶h̶ ̶'
Nick Leslau, leading property entrepreneur and Channel 4
Secret Millionaire

'*The spirit of NLP is building models of success, in this case successful decision making. This book can help us have a better understanding of our own process when making important decisions and even more help us make decisions that are based in some wisdom and ecology.*'

Judith Delozier, NLP founder

'Brilliant Decision Making *takes you on a fascinating journey inside your own mind. Now you can understand how to make great decisions that make a difference in your life.*'

Shelle Rose Charvet, author of *Words That Change Minds* and *The Customer is Bothering Me*

'*Good decisions lie at the heart of any successful business – this book provides an excellent framework for making decisions, and more importantly, how to refine those decisions to make sure they actually work out.*'

Mike Southon, *Financial Times* columnist and co-author of *The Beermat Entrepreneur*

'*Robbie has a highly original life philosophy and is a talented businessman, NLP coach, and drummer! His new book is a good read and presents a clear framework for successful decision making both for business and for life.*'

Frank Pennal, Managing Director, Close Property Finance Ltd – Close Broth̶e̶r̶s̶ ̶B̶a̶n̶k̶

90

'*This is a first-rate field-guide that demystifies decision making for everyone. Written with expert insight, powerful examples and bucketloads of practical know-how, this is a book to help you make more smart decisions more often in all areas of your life. Highly recommended.*'

Francis Currie, International Medial Consultancy and previously Managing Director of Heart FM

'*Robbie demystifies the decision-making process in a way that combines empirical research, psychology and straightforward business savvy. Buy this book if you're serious about increasing the effectiveness of your decisions.*'

Donald MacNaughton, Olympic and Football Premier league coach

'*This is a worthwhile book for anybody who wants to make better decisions. Combining NLP with Robbie's own personal, highly practical, tips – it's a useful addition to any bookshelf.*'

Kimberley Hare, CEO Kaizen Training Limited

'Brilliant Decision Making *is long overdue. We make decisions every day of our lives in business and in private yet we never get trained to make them. Robbie brings both his experience as a successful entrepreneur and a leading business coach to the subject and delivers simple and clear guidance. This book will help everyone who reads it.*'

Andy Hawkes, CEO THB UK Limited

'*I really like this book. It's certainly got me thinking about how I tend to make decisions too quickly!*'

Amanda Vickers, MD of Speak First and author of *Personal Impact* and *Teach Yourself NLP* and *Coaching*

brilliant

decision making

decision making

What the best decision makers know, do and say

Robbie Steinhouse

Prentice Hall
is an imprint of

Harlow, England • London • New York • Boston • San Francisco • Toronto • Sydney • Singapore • Hong Kong
Tokyo • Seoul • Taipei • New Delhi • Cape Town • Madrid • Mexico City • Amsterdam • Munich • Paris • Milan

PEARSON EDUCATION LIMITED

Edinburgh Gate
Harlow CM20 2JE
Tel: +44 (0)1279 623623
Fax: +44 (0)1279 431059
Website: www.pearsoned.

First published in Great 2010

2010 © Robert Steinhouse 2010

The right of Robert Steinhouse to be identified as author of this work has been
asserted by him in accordance with the Copyright,
1988.

ISBN: 978-0-273-73414-7

British Library Cataloguing-in-Publication Data
A catalogue record for this book is available from the British Library

Library of Congress Cataloging-in-Publication Data
Steinhouse, Robbie.
    Brilliant decsion making : what the best decision makers know, do and say /
Robbie Steinhouse.
         p. cm.
    Includes index.
    ISBN 978-0-273-73414-7 (pbk.)
    1. Decision making.   I. Title.
    BF448.s74 2010
    153.8'3--dc22

                                                                    2009052031

10 9 8 7 6 5 4 3 2 1
14 13 12 11 10

Illustrations by Bill Piggins

Typeset in 10/14pt Plantin by 3
Printed in Great Britain by Henry Ling Ltd., at the Dorset Press, Dorchester,
Dorset

The publisher's policy is to use paper manufactured from sustainable forests.

Contents

About the author

Robbie Steinhouse is co-author of *Think Like an Entrepreneur* and a successful serial entrepreneur. Over the past 25 years he has founded and built businesses in the property, recruitment and insurance sectors. He is also head of training at NLP School Europe, a certified NLP trainer, an ICF certified coach and managing director of the Coaching Consultancy.

Acknowledgements

I would like to dedicate this book to my wife Chii and daughters Natalie and Emily. They have all been most supportive of – OK, and occasionally made fun of – my endless talking about this subject.

I would also like to thank everyone at Pearson, especially my commissioning editor Samantha Jackson for her patience in developing the ideas through many incarnations, as well as Caroline Jordan, Natasha Whelan and Lucy Blackmore.

The co-author of my last book, Chris West, also helped me edit this book, coached me on how to write and generally guided me through the process. He even came up with some rather good ideas. If you want to write a book, I can't recommend him highly enough: his e-mail address is chris@chriswest.info

Lastly, I would like to thank everyone who has helped me learn how to make decisions: my business clients, business partners, staff, NLP students, coaching clients and NLP teachers, especially Robert Dilts. Being part of their journeys has given me much access to brilliant decision making in action.

Authors like to hear from readers: if you find this book helpful but want to ask further questions (or just comment), do get in touch. My e-mail is robbie@nlpschool.com – I look forward to hearing from you.

Introduction

'*Every great leap forward in your life comes after you have made a clear decision of some kind.*'

Brian Tracy, Canadian writer and professional speaker

I love that quote. It sums up for me what decision making is all about: change and progress. Decisions set us free. Decisions give us control over our own lives. Decisions are the most powerful form of self-expression available to each and every one of us; they turn our most cherished personal values into real living forces in the world. The art of deciding lies at the heart of the art of living.

But there's an unattractive myth that goes alongside this: that decision making is some kind of innate skill we either have or don't have, that we are either born 'decisive' or 'indecisive', and that we are stuck with this trait from then on, like height or natural eye colour.

Wrong!

We can *all* learn how to make brilliant decisions, by being taught how to do it well, and by getting out there and practising the art.

Sadly, people can also learn how to make bad decisions (or not make decisions at all), by being given false information about decision making or by learning the wrong lessons from their own (or others') experience. This may have happened to you – never mind, it's now time to *un*learn all that old stuff and set off on the road to becoming the brilliant decision maker you have a right to be.

I'd like to zap a couple more myths about decision making before we start our journey.

First, the myth of 'decisiveness'. This is often trumpeted as what decision making is 'all about'. But it isn't. This is because it implies quick decision making – but important decisions need time: if you rush into them too fast, thinking that by doing so you are being 'decisive', you are actually limiting your decision-making potential.

Clearly some decisions must be made quickly, and then decisiveness – coming to a clear decision fast – is important. But with larger decisions, the long-term ones that shape our lives, flexibility and insight are much more important. A measure of decisiveness is part of the brilliant decision maker's armoury, but only a part, and he or she knows when to deploy it and when not to.

Second, there is a myth that big decisions hinge on one critical moment. But decisions of any size are *processes*, that begin with an awareness of the need for change and end long after, when you finally secure a set of 'outcomes'. During this process, you have to make lots of decisions, not just one.

Yes, there is almost always a central decision at the heart of the process, but even with these, the art of brilliant decision making lies in leaving doors open for as long as possible; in other words, lessening the critical nature of the big, central decision.

There is also a process of building up to the central decision – and during this you will usually have to make smaller, 'mini-decisions'. Sometimes these will make the central decision easy, or even redundant. And, of course, the decision-making process also continues after the central one, not just as 'implementation' but as more decisions.

One more point I'd like to make here: although all decision making creates progress, it is not a guarantee of specific outcomes. Often the progress is not what you expected – but it is progress nonetheless, without which life becomes stale.

So let's set off on the journey towards mastering the art of brilliant decision making, and towards the power, freedom, responsibility and enjoyment of life that such mastery brings with it.

Getting the best from this book

I begin in Part 1 with a brief overview of the psychology of decision making: how the brain actually works as we decide. Neuroscience is getting ever better at observing the brain in action, and the results are fascinating – overturning centuries of received wisdom.

I shall then look at different types of decision in the light of the above discoveries. (Want to know how the world's greatest chess player chooses his moves? Find out here!)

The heart of the book, Part 2, follows: my four-stage process for brilliant decision making. I developed this over many years of building a successful business, but I have found that it works well in other areas of life. I am now a busy coach, and my clients bring issues of every imaginable kind to me, almost all of which seem to benefit from the application of this process.

The process can be broken down simply into:

1 A quick run-through of the issue in hand, in what I call the 'decision simulator'.

2 Preparing for the central decision.

3 Making the central decision.

4 Putting the decision into practice.

After that, I will present a troubleshooting guide. This is something to be used at any time in the four-stage process when you feel stuck.

The rest of the book, Part 3, is taken up with 'contexts': observations on those aspects of decision making that I think are most important to understand if you are to master the art.

The first of these is practice. Brilliant decision making is an art that can be learnt. But how exactly do you do this?

Next, I look at how decision making applies to all areas of life: career, relationships, family, money, health, lifestyle, the search for inner peace ... However, people often have an 'Achilles' heel'. Many people who are fundamentally good decision makers in most areas allow poor decision making in one or two other areas to become the dominant negative force in their lives, threatening to undo all the good work they do. How can this be avoided?

I shall talk a little about making decisions in groups. The focus of this book is on the individual decision maker, but you may well find yourself in a group decision-making situation. In which case, here is my advice.

Finally, I draw a parallel between the journey of decision making and the 'heroic journey' used by storytellers (and Hollywood scriptwriters). The parallels are illuminating and can be inspirational.

I recommend reading the book through to the end first, then dipping into it whenever you feel the need to remind yourself of a particular aspect – such as the four-stage process, which you will probably not commit to memory first time, but which will, if you use it regularly, become instinctive.

I would like to add a note about NLP. This is a school of psychology and personal development that I have studied for many years and now teach. The letters stand for Neuro-Linguistic Programming, which is a rather grand way of saying that NLP looks at the way we programme our minds using various languages (words, obviously, but also other 'languages' – of image, sound, gesture, emotions . . .). This programming is done auto-matically, and rather haphazardly, as we grow up: as adults, we can do a better job and reprogramme our minds to get us what we want – now.

I will be using NLP from time to time in the material that follows. However, rest assured that you need *no* previous know-ledge of NLP to get the best out of this book and I shan't be bombarding you with NLP terms.

PART 1

Understanding decision making

CHAPTER 1

The psychology of decision making

A master of any craft understands the tools he or she uses, and your main tool as a brilliant decision maker is your brain. So I would like to take a brief look at psychology and neurology in those areas relevant to decision making.

The work that our unconscious mind gets on with can be highly complex: brain scans have been run on individuals while they are making decisions, and show a kind of inner debate going on. Different parts of the brain become activated, like people standing up in a debating chamber and having their say (though rather faster than most debaters). This happens 'out of awareness': the person making the decisions doesn't know this is going on.

brilliant definition

The unconscious mind

The brain does most of its work without our being aware of the fact. For example, it regulates our breathing without us giving it any conscious orders to do so. But the same is also true of our 'higher' mental faculties: the phenomenon of 'sleeping on a problem' shows that the brain works away at problems without conscious interference (and usually does better when we switch our conscious mind off).

Other experiments have shown that the brain even makes decisions before the brain's owner is aware of the fact. Back in the 1980s, research at the University of California, San Francisco, showed that simple decisions (the example used was when to move a finger in response to a stimulus) were made about three-tenths of a second before the individual was aware of their decision. More recently this time lag has been shown to apply to more complex problem-solving. Two researchers, at London's Goldsmiths College and at the University of Houston, set students a lateral thinking test. They monitored brain activity and found sudden waves of a particular kind in the right frontal cortex (a part of the brain that solves problems) *eight seconds* before an answer was produced 'consciously' – and no such waves in the brains of those who didn't come up with an answer.

brilliant tip

Our unconscious mind is a fantastic machine for making decisions.

It is believed that our ancestors of 50,000 years ago had neither language nor self-awareness. However, they were clearly able to perform complex activities like hunting in groups, making tools or looking after children, all of which involve making decisions. Imagine an ancestor out hunting. He makes loads of decisions based on past experience and what he has observed. Where should he stand to ambush his prey? Where should he stick the spear to ensure a good, clean kill? He doesn't go through a conscious thought process – 'Hmm, that tree's a bit sparse. The antelope might spot me. But if I hide behind that bush, it might get away . . .' But his mind assesses these options and he makes a decision – which has to be a good one, or he and his family go hungry.

Our unconscious mind is not perfect, however. Research has shown that it has weak points, based around the role of emotions in decisions. There are three main situations where this is the case.

The first category is decisions about immediate gratification. The unconscious mind is biased towards short-term pleasures. While it has the ability to consider long-term consequences, this ability gets overridden by the lure of the delicious and immediately available. This has been demonstrated scientifically – though anyone on a diet faced with a slice of chocolate cake could have told the scientists that was the case.

> the unconscious mind is biased towards short-term pleasures

By contrast, in long-term decision making the unconscious mind has a tendency to worry too much about the pain of loss. This 'loss aversion', which was discovered by the psychologists Kahneman and Tversky (the big names in the academic study of decision making), means in essence that the unconscious is conservative. We let what we stand to lose by making a decision get in the way of what we stand to gain by making it. As most decisions involve losing something, if we are very 'loss averse' then we can become paralysed, and turn away from enormous potential gains because of fear of relatively small losses.

brilliant example

- Investors often hold on to stocks that are clearly in trouble, because they don't want to make a loss on them, even though the rational thing to do would be to accept the loss and reinvest whatever money is left in a stock with better prospects.

- People in dysfunctional relationships often remain trapped in there for years because they are afraid of what might go wrong if they got out.

The third way in which our unconscious mind can let us down is in those situations where we have to make an urgent decision in an area where we are unfamiliar. The problem here is another kind of overload: the 'fight or flight' response kicks in, when actually what we need to do is stop and think things through – even for a moment.

brilliant example

In scuba diving, when learners get into difficulty their instinct is often 'flight': to rush up to the surface as quickly as possible. But that can be fatal. It is drummed into trainee divers that they must override their flight reaction and give their reason as much time as possible to work out a better solution.

On the other hand, urgent decisions in areas where we are experts are much better left to the unconscious mind – I shall talk more about this later.

So, is emotion damaging to decision making? No. Research shows that it is an essential part of it. People who have suffered brain damage that renders them unable to feel emotion also become helplessly indecisive, endlessly vacillating between options in even the tiniest decision. It seems that a decision is a fascinating mixture of emotion and reason, and that much deciding is done at the unconscious level.

> a decision is a fascinating mixture of emotion and reason

These insights are radically different from the traditional view of how we direct our lives. This held that the unconscious, emotional mind was last year's model, which had largely been superseded by the new model – the conscious, rational mind. The emotional mind was now actually a bit of a nuisance. We'd

be better off without it! The Greek philosopher Plato saw the psyche as a two-horse chariot. One horse is wild, wilful and destructive – our negative emotions. The other is pretty wild, too, but affectionate and benevolent – our nicer emotions. In charge of these moody, argumentative and powerful beasts is a charioteer: our conscious reason. Reason has to whip the horses into line and try and keep them heading in what the charioteer has decided is the 'right' direction. It's not an easy job, and charioteers often feel that the horses are their enemy . . .

This was not just a view in ancient Greece. It has been the received wisdom of intelligent people until very recently. Even so-called 'trail-blazing' thinkers like Freud essentially subscribed to it.

But it's wrong! The horses may have the power described by Plato, but they are actually very savvy. As a general rule, they want to – and have learnt how to – pull the chariot in a healthy, useful direction. Wise charioteers understand this and teach themselves to work with them. They may guide the horses in new directions, but they let the horses learn the details of and decide the exact routes to take. However, in three circumstances (described above), emotions can 'short circuit' the system, forcing an unwise decision: in these cases, where the otherwise sensible horses get 'spooked' (and only in those cases), Plato's model still holds good.

This book is all about how to use your reason and intelligence to direct the marvellous decision-making machine that is your unconscious mind. Much of this skill lies in letting the unconscious mind get on with it – but not all. *Brilliant decisions arise out of the managed interplay between conscious and unconscious mindwork.*

Maybe a better model than Plato's charioteer is that of craft experts, such as carpenters or dressmakers. They have a range of tools at their disposal – in the decision maker's case it is reason, intuition, emotion, experience, courage, imagination – and know what tool to use, and when and how.

Exactly how do you master this craft? Read on . . .

What kind of decision maker are you?

Have a go at this light-hearted quiz. You can be more than one of these decision makers – most important, ask yourself which ones you would like to be.

Tortoises take ages to make decisions. However, the decisions they make are often good ones. Slowly but steadily they advance towards their goals.

Hares are the sort of people we regard as 'decisive'. They always seem to be making decisions. However, their decisions are often made too hastily – they have this belief that the quicker the decision, the more 'decisive' they are seen as being. But actually a lot of their decisions are poor ones, based on inadequate information about themselves or the relevant facts out there.

Hippos are slow decision makers, or non-decision makers, who seem to love wallowing in the mud of indecision. They often play the 'victim': 'Look at me, stuck in all this mud. It's all right for you up there on dry land' (etc., etc.). They could, of course, decide to crawl out of the mud, but somehow they just never get round to it . . .

Rabbits (in headlights) just freeze when they have to make a decision. They don't enjoy indecision in the way that hippos seem to – they're just petrified.

Ostriches avoid decisions by hiding their heads in the sand and pretending the need for the decision will go away.

Magpies find decision making difficult in the face of bright, shiny objects that they just have to have, whether they really need them or not.

Flipper, that lovable dolphin, makes decisions in two ways. He makes a load of decisions, very quickly. Then, exhausted, he enters a phase of making none at all – till the pressure builds up to make more, when he becomes hyper-decisive again. This cycle keeps going round and round.

Eagles keep a keen eye on the landscape below them. When they see that something needs to be done, they act in a timely fashion.

Macaques are supposed to be the most intelligent of all non-human animals: they can learn complex behaviours from each other, as well as from their own mistakes.

CHAPTER 2

Types of decision and how to make them brilliantly

There are many types of decision. This chapter looks at a number of these in the light of the psychological material above.

Big, long-term decisions with enough time

The main focus of this book is on big life-changing decisions, where we grab control of our lives and say to whatever forces that have been keeping us poor, lonely, unfit (or whatever): 'Enough is enough. I'm taking over my life now!'

I also include substantial purchase decisions in this category – a house, a car . . .

For these decisions, I have a four-stage process, which will be outlined in the following chapters.

Big, long-term decisions with little time

Are you *sure* you can't buy a bit more time? There's advice on buying time in Stage 2 of the material that follows (see Chapter 4). Remember the proverb 'Marry in haste, repent at leisure'.

If the answer really is 'No, my time is fixed and short', then use the first part of the process that follows – the 'decision simulator' – and as much of the rest of the process as you have time for.

Most of this book will be about the above two types of decision, because they are the ones that matter most. However, before I get into the details of how we handle these as brilliantly as possible, I would like to comment on other types of decision, which, although less substantial, can still impact on our lives.

Snap decisions, of all levels of importance

Some decisions have to be made in a moment: snap decisions. There are essentially two kinds of these: ones in areas where we have a lot of experience, and ones where we are confronted with something totally new.

Where we have experience, our unconscious mind will have been doing lots of learning, and it's almost always best to go with 'gut feel' or intuition. Most issues involving the assessment of our fellow human beings fall into this category: our brains have been learning how to do this since we were born (and no doubt have innate mechanisms for this, too).

> it's almost always best to go with 'gut feel' or intuition

Garry Kasparov, arguably the greatest chess player ever, plays purely by intuition ('I play by smell, by feel'). Of course, he practises endlessly, playing thousands of games and – most interesting of all – minutely analysing any mistakes he has made. He does this not to beat himself up but to make sure the message of what he did wrong goes into his unconscious mind, which then knows not to do it again.

Poker is another good example of gut feel at work. Professionals use their reason to master the mathematics of probability. But at the same time, they use their intuition to 'suss out' the other players at the table. It is this intuitive, unconscious skill that enables them to make the instant decisions that win or lose fortunes at the poker table. When I pressed Al Alvarez, a writer who has played the game for many years, on exactly how he made these judgements, he said he didn't know. 'You just get a feel for how people are playing.'

A more tricky issue arises when we have to make a snap decision in response to *some totally new challenge*, where our old patterns and models just won't work. For example, what would the poker pros do if the casino caught fire? Our instinct here is often 'fight or flight'.

The right way to decide here is the one taught to the scuba divers: override instinct, for a moment at least, and give yourself a tiny space to think your predicament through. If you can do this, your brain will work incredibly fast to come up with alternatives.

 **tip**

For snap decisions in familiar territory. Learn all you can beforehand. Then follow your gut feel.

For snap decisions in unfamiliar territory. Stop. Think. Act.

Decisions about immediate gratification

These are often quick decisions, though not as 'snap' as someone faced with an emergency or a chess player challenged by their opponent's last move.

Reason needs to take control. Ask yourself: 'What are the consequences of indulging?'

If you find yourself regularly in a situation where you are tempted to act in a way that is against your long-term better interest, develop a 'counterweight'. It can be a memory, a picture, a sound, a feeling, a smell – anything that pulls you in the opposite direction to the temptation.

Tricia has decided to lose weight. She has an image that she brings to mind whenever she sees some particularly tempting but unhealthy food – of a very overweight person struggling to carry some shopping. 'That's me, if I start eating stuff like this again', she says to herself, and the craving is outweighed.

If the temptation is less of a problem (I'm a great believer in the old music-hall adage, that 'A little of what you fancy does you good'), then just ask a quick question: 'Am I willing to accept the consequences of this?' If you still want to go ahead, great – just check in with yourself quickly first!

NLP teaches that many people move through phases of temptation. They begin with a relatively gentle 'would like it' phase, then escalate to a relentless 'must have it' phase. You will be most effective in controlling gratification impulses if you act early on.

One area of gratification that can be very irrational is our desire for risk. As with all potentially damaging behaviour, we need to protect ourselves from sudden, overwhelming desires to take silly risks, but not at the expense of making life dull.

For gratification decisions: Stop. Are consequences reasonable? Decide.

Decisions where fear of loss weighs heavily

Here you need to do some rational calculations of pros and cons. Then keep reminding yourself of them.

Take time to 'craft' a good decision. Use the four-stage process, and keep reminding yourself of the positive outcomes that the decision will bring you.

Watch out for 'buyer's remorse' (see page 86) if you decide to act. But remember that this emotion is a passing phase. Remember, also, the old saying: 'Fortune favours the brave'.

Decisions where you have too much time and do too much thinking

In the above examples, I've shown that the unconscious mind can be unbalanced by emotion, and a bit of whip-cracking by the 'charioteer' of reason is required. However, some-times the decision process can be unbalanced by too much reason.

> sometimes the decision process can be unbalanced by too much reason

Too much reasoning can lead to the phenomenon called 'chok-ing' in sport, where people who have mastered brilliant body moves like a golf swing or a tennis serve suddenly start thinking too much about what they are doing and lose the skill. In these cases, you must silence your reason. Either concentrate on something else, or have a word like 'flowing' or 'easy' to concen-trate on.

Reason can also damage longer-term decision making through the phenomenon of 'rumination', whereby people who have undergone a negative experience force their minds to go over and over it in a totally passive way. But they don't learn anything from this – unlike Garry Kasparov learning from his mistakes in chess matches. They just get stuck in a kind of loop, endlessly reliving the experience and not doing anything about the consequences of it. Many psychologists regard this as a major cause of depression. A big decision to change some area of your life is the best antidote to this that I know.

I know of someone who consistently accepted more and more bizarre behaviour from his partner and became more and more angry and upset – but did nothing about it, just ruminated. At one point I was asked, 'Do you think it reasonable that she wants to go out with other men as friends, but will not let me come along?' I answered that he had the right at least to have an invitation to go along too, and suggested he test the situation out by saying this. He did, and she refused. He just accepted this. Had he made a decision that certain behaviour would not be tolerated, things would either have got better or she would have gone off in a huff. But they just dragged on in this misery. In the end, she eventually got fed up and left him. Later I asked him if he had learnt anything from the whole affair, at which point he said, 'No, not really'.

'Act or be acted upon.'

Stephen Covey, American writer

The best thing to do when stuck in rumination is to give yourself a deadline by which you have to take some action. This will get your unconscious mind out of the loop it has got stuck in and get it considering alternative futures.

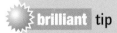 **brilliant** tip

Thinking about it too much and can't decide? Give yourself a deadline and stick to it.

↗ brilliant recap

Different types of decision and how to deal with them:

- Big, long-term decisions: use this book's four-stage process for brilliant decision making.

- Big decisions that you truly need to make quickly: use the decision simulator, the first part of the four-stage process, and as much of the rest of the process as you have time for.

- Snap decisions in areas where you have experience (this includes assessing people): trust your intuition.

- Snap decisions forced by a totally new challenge: give yourself a tiny space to think things through consciously.

- Decisions about immediate gratification: give yourself a tiny space to weigh up the consequences of your action. If it is a regular problem, have a counterweight.

- Decisions where fear of loss weighs heavily: stick to the four-stage process and don't be sidetracked.

- Decisions where you have too much time and start ruminating: give yourself a deadline for action.

PART 2

The brilliant decision-making process

T his, as I have said, is a process for important decisions. Such decisions are usually complex and require time – to set up, to make and to implement.

Because of this, I have broken the process down into three stages of preparing, making and implementing. A fourth stage comes before any of these – a brief ride in what I call the 'decision simulator'. This is a quick, and hugely useful, way of bringing clarity to an issue on which a decision needs to be made. Even at the earliest stages of considering a decision, we usually have an awareness of options for action in our minds, albeit (at this point) ill-formed and ill-understood ones. Run these quickly through this simulator and see what happens.

The simulator is not a substitute for a thorough decision-making process – it is a gateway into such a process. However, it can be used as a decision-making tool in its own right in instances where the decision is not major or where time is tight.

Following on from the four-step process, I present a trouble-shooting guide. This is something to refer to if at any time during the process you suddenly find yourself stuck, unable to decide, troubled, or undergoing any other kind of psychological stress.

CHAPTER 3

Stage 1: The decision simulator

From the 1940s to the 1980s the proportion of plane crashes caused by pilot error remained constant at approximately 65 per cent. In the 1980s flight simulators became part of pilot training, so pilots could learn to make life or death decisions in a safe environment. By 2009 the proportion of plane crashes due to pilot error had dropped to under 30 per cent.

The 'decision simulator' is a chance to experiment quite quickly in your mind with potential courses of action. You may emerge from it with a clear view of what you want – but, unless you really have no time, do not regard this as a final decision. A provisional one, maybe . . . More likely, you will emerge with a vague idea of where you want to get to and of some of the issues you might have to deal with on your way to that point. If you get either of those outcomes, the simulator has done a great job, and it will be time to move on to Stage 2, when you get into the nuts and bolts of turning these vague ideas into a clear, specific, powerful, detailed decision.

But for now, just strap on your seat belts and let me take you on a journey . . .

Essentially, the decision simulator involves asking yourself eight powerful questions:

1 What is the decision I face?
2 So, what am I going to do?
3 What do I want to happen?
4 How will I know when it has happened?
5 Why is the decision important to me?
6 What could go wrong? And what could I do about that?
7 What are the first three steps?
8 Where have I got to now?

Let's look at the questions one by one and consider why they are as they are and what you can expect from them. As we do this, we shall eavesdrop. on Amit, who has been offered a job in Germany and has to decide whether to take it or not.

What is the decision I face?

Amit writes down: 'I have been offered this job in Germany. Should I take it?'

In doing this, he has already set his unconscious mind working on the issue.

So, what am I going to do?

The great thing about the simulator is that it isn't reality. If you've ever been in a real flight simulator, you soon forget this fact and start sweating and shuddering as your 'aeroplane' hurtles to the ground – while all the time you are actually sitting in a little plastic seat in front of a set of screens. So it is in your decision simulator. You can decide anything you like. It's all in your head; nobody else need know, but your experience of the decision will be startlingly realistic.

You can run the simulator with a number of choices. Personally, I find it helpful to run it with whatever option is my 'front runner' at the time, but I don't see this as an absolute rule. Many decisions are two-pronged (dyadic, to use the technical term) – 'either I do x or I do y', or 'I'll do x or nothing' – in which case, why not run both?

Amit decides to run with the decision: 'Yes, I'm taking that job!'

What do I want to happen?

Amit replies, 'I want to get a job that represents real promotion, but without upsetting my family, which might happen if I relocate to another country'.

This is a good answer, but an even better answer would have been: 'I want to get a job that represents a real promotion, while keeping my family happy and united.' The difference is that in the second reply both 'arms' of what Amit wants are expressed in the positive.

The purpose of this question is to focus the unconscious mind on positive outcomes. This is hugely important. Focus on what you want, and your mind will start working towards getting it. Focus on what you don't want, and you'll be stuck with that negative picture and no clear route out.

> focus on what you want, and your mind will start working towards getting it

How will I know when it has happened?

Amit has set himself a positive goal. But it's still a bit general. This next question makes your goals much more specific.

A well known concept is that of the SMART outcome. This is an outcome that is:

- **S**pecific
- **M**easurable
- **A**chievable
- **R**esourced
- **T**imed.

'Resourced' is the one most people stumble on. Have you got the resources you need – of time, of money, of energy, of support – to make the outcome happen? If not, how are you going to get these?

---

brilliant example

Nick sets himself the goal of getting rid of all his debt (apart from a mortgage on a property) in five years. At the same time, he intends to be earning £30,000 a year. He can 'resource' this decision by talking to friends who have got better-paying jobs, by consulting the local careers guidance service and by taking a correspondence course in whatever area of work he decides to master.

SMART goals are hugely powerful. However, I believe you should take the concept even further. Give yourself clear evidence of what achieving a goal would be like: what would you actually experience when you had done this? Although this may seem obvious, people often don't have a clear idea of what success would look or feel like. Ask yourself:

- What specifically will I *see* when I have this goal?
- What specifically will I *hear* when I have this goal?
- What specifically will I *feel* when I have this goal?

Amit imagines sitting in an office chair and feeling the pleasure that comes from doing a good job and knowing it.

Getting down to this level of specificity enables us to harness the power of visualisation:

Imagine that you have your outcome already. Now let yourself experience all the feelings, pictures and sounds that go with it . . .

You are creating an unconscious destination for yourself: once you have put in your brain a really clear image of what you want to achieve, there will be part of you which, like the automatic pilot on a plane, will know where it's heading and will be able to move you towards that image with greater ease and elegance.

This is the theme of many books like Rhonda Byrne's *The Secret*.

Using meditation and visualisation

Here are three brief visualisations for health, money and relationships. Begin each of the visualisations with the relaxation meditation that comes before them. They are all best listened to rather than read – some of the grammar is a bit funny, but this is deliberate. Get a friend to read them to you, or record yourself reading them, or download an MP3 of my reading them from my website: www.brilliantdecisionmaking.com

It is probably better to do just one of the visualisations in a session rather than to cram two or three in.

Relaxation meditation

Take a little time to settle yourself and become aware of your breathing. Allow yourself to become settled, allowing your body to be fully

supported by the ground. Wherever you are right now – just let go. You don't need to think about anything; you don't need to do anything; just allow yourself to be as you are, right now. Letting go of wanting to change or control things; just allow yourself to be as you are, right now. Just focus on your breathing and notice how your mind begins to quiet…

Now go to one of the visualisations below:

Health visualisation

Imagine you have that feeling of healthy vitality you did when you were young. Imagine having that sense of movement, that sense of ease, that sense of … health. That's right, allow yourself to fully experience health right now. Imagine seeing yourself in a mirror: how will your body look? Imagine the look on your face – of triumph, of contentment? Notice your breathing, how does it sound? And notice your body … Allow yourself to remember again that feeling of vitality of energy; no more pains, just the power of a fit body; and notice what you are saying to yourself and what you have stopped saying to yourself. Just allow yourself to imagine that right now. And now imagine having that at your chosen future date …

Wealth visualisation

Imagine the day that you know you have enough money to feel secure for your future. Imagine how you would find that out; who would tell you or would you read it somewhere? Become aware of the new feelings you have and anything you are saying to yourself. Notice how the old feelings are gone and the words you used to say to yourself don't matter any more. Fully experience the positive feelings of having all the money you want right now – that's right, what is it like to have this feeling? Dare to have it, why not – just for a little while. And you can make it even stronger.

Relationship visualisation

Imagine having a sense of ease and connection with another person. A sense of intimacy and security. Allow yourself to simply

*enjoy the sense of the ending of the search and knowing it was all
worth it. This may have been a long journey, but right now you have
a sense of someone loving you and a sense of loving in your life. You
can have this feeling without the need of another; you can simply
experience this light feeling of love and joy – and feeling that right
now, you know that this will make you feel more attractive and
attract others to stay in your life. Have that sense of independence
ready to greet another's independence – to produce something, new
and wonderful. Allow yourself to fully experience this right now.*

Why is the decision important to me?

Decisions have many contexts. The most important of these is
that of your own values and purpose. How will this decision help
you get to where you really want to get to in your life? By what
ultimate criteria will you judge its success or failure?

Ask yourself these questions:

A If I took that decision and it worked out, what would that
    do for me personally?

B Knowing that, what would that enable me to experience
    that is even more important or bigger?

Don't just ask these questions once. Keep 'looping' round question B until you get to an answer that
seems complete in itself, that needs
no justification. Each time you loop
around, pause for a few moments
and actually experience the sensa-
tions that go with your answer.

> pause for a few
> moments and actually
> experience the
> sensations that go with
> your answer

Usually when people are asked to
make a decision that will help them with *external* things like
career or money, looping round question B a few times leads

them to *internal* goals, to the hope that they will feel different in some way – for example 'happy' or 'relaxed'. Carrying on further with question B often then leads beyond these relatively simple states to more sophisticated ones, which are deeper, more lasting and often more spiritual.

Amit simply answers question A with 'I'd be progressing in my career'.

The first time he answers question B he talks about being more respected in the company. What would that do for him? Pride. What would that do for him? Something to do with showing his father how much he could achieve. And what would that do for him? Repay his father's love. And that? Make him more loving towards his own family. And that? He would be fulfilling his role as a human being. And that? At that point, Amit finds he can't go any further; he has found an end truly worth pursuing in itself. This is, of course, a fine discovery in itself, let alone its use-fulness in helping him make his decision.

The point of this is to discover if the decision you took in answer to the second of the eight questions ('So, what am I going to do?') really does fit with your higher purposes in life. If it does, then that's great. If not, what changes do you need to make?

---

brilliant example

Sarah simulated her decision to buy a new car. One of those four-wheel drive things, that put you up above the rest of the traffic. What would that do for her? She said it would provide her with a sense of accomplishment. And what would that do for her? She said it would make her feel more relaxed. And what would that do for her? It would make her feel at one with all things. Suddenly the idea of a gas-guzzling giant and the huge monthly payments she'd need to make to pay for it completely clashed with wanting to feel at one with all things. She decided to keep her Nissan Micra and buy a bike for popping down to the shops.

At other times, the decision can simply lose its urgency.

 **example**

Neil wanted to buy a car for his wife, and became worried about getting the right brand. Asking himself why the decision was important showed that his deeper motive was to show his love for his wife – which he could do in plenty of other ways. The emotional content was removed from the decision: he then went round to his local dealer, a man he knew and trusted, and bought a car straight away (his wife, who has no interest in car brands anyway, loves it).

Doing this exercise will also help the 'automatic pilot' we set up with the last question. If your decision leads to deeper outcomes that you really want, you now have a powerful new motivator alongside those visible, audible, tangible signs of success.

Some people tend to be motivated by big visions; others prefer to concentrate on details. You now have both kinds of motivator working for you.

What could go wrong? And what could I do about that?

You've taken your decision. Now come up with four negative scenarios – four things that could really go wrong as a result of it. Be realistic rather than fanciful.

Then think of what you could do to prevent them happening or to minimise their effects if they did happen.

Amit immediately thinks of his family. His wife might be unhappy – she doesn't speak German and isn't a brilliant linguist. Supposing the kids didn't settle in the local schools? And then supposing the new job didn't work out – however good you

are, you can have personality clashes that mess things up. And –
a relatively trivial thought pops into his head as he is answering,
but his unconscious has provided it so he must respect it – supposing I hate the food there? Don't they eat loads of sausages
and meat in Germany? I'm a vegetarian!

One of the reasons people fail to make decisions and instead
think a problem over and over (and over and over . . .) is because
some part of them doesn't feel comfortable about making that
decision. Some fear is stopping them. This question gives you a
chance to look at what's stopping you and if it is a real 'deal
breaker' or something that can be worked around.

Remember that there are essentially two types of criticism:

- *Positive criticism* is about protection – spotting potential
  pitfalls and making sure something is done about them.
- *Negative criticism* is about spoiling – pointless sniping at
  good ideas, which achieves nothing.

The two activities can look similar, but are very different. It's all
about the motivation of the critic. This section is about positive
criticism!

The most creative part of us can often come through being
critical. If we are able to be critical without being a spoiler, to put
that negative voice away and just focus on the protective voice,
this can open a huge seam of creativity and lead on to greatly
improved planning and decision making.

Amit needs to look through his four objections. They are all
rational. Fine. The next thing to do is to come up with plans to
get round the problems. For
example, he can find out how big an
expat community there is in the city
he is being asked to move to. Can he
find out about schools at the same time? The problem with the
job not working out may need addressing by some mentoring to

> come up with plans to
> get round the problems

boost his confidence, and by his keeping an eye open for difficult individuals when he starts and nipping any problems in the bud. The food question is easily solved by talking to a friend who'd been to Berlin and who can assure him there are plenty of vegetarian restaurants (and restaurants of all kinds) in modern Germany.

To recap:

- List four things that could go wrong.
- Sort out any irrational fears.
- For the rational fears, ask (of each one) 'What am I going to do about this?' Come up with practical alternatives that will reduce the risk of its happening.

What are the first three steps?

Ask three questions:

- What is the first step I must take to move myself towards my outcome?
- What is the next step after that?
- What is the next step after that?

We have largely looked at outcomes so far, but these are only reached by courses of action, initiated in the right sequence. This question will really get you moving: putting your plan into action (even in a simulator) puts your mind into gear.

Sometimes an outcome can look, sound and feel great, fit bigger values and not have any 'critic' objections that you cannot get round – but still can be incredibly hard to reach.

Amit writes down:

- Find out about expat community.
- Find out about schools.

- Talk to Keith in Leicester office who has worked in Frankfurt office and knows the people there.

Someone with a less precise, more 'visionary' mind might well bundle all this under:

- Get more information.

This is too broad. Break it down further. Obviously I don't mean:

- Check number of Leicester office.
- Dial number.
- Ask if Keith is there.

Use your common sense here! (This may sound an obvious point, but in coaching I find that clients often first come up with tiny steps, which are not enough to really get the unconscious mind working on the question 'How am I actually going to get to my outcome?')

Where have I got to now?

Now it is time to do a check on the decision you took into the simulator and your chosen outcomes. Ask yourself if they seem right at three levels: head, heart and gut? Or, more specifically:

- At the level of my *head*, thinking now, do I think that the decision has a realistic chance of working out? And, if so, do I really have the time and money to commit to it now or soon?
- At the level of my *heart*, feeling now, is this something that I really want to do?
- At the level of my *gut*, do I really believe that I am the sort of person who is going to make this decision and follow it through? Am I allowed to do this kind of thing? And do I deserve the outcomes?

Don't worry about the formulation of the questions – there's a reason for how they are the way they are. Right now, just ask, and see what answers your unconscious mind comes up with.

Amit ends up in a positive mood about his decision. It makes sense intellectually. It feels good, though he has worries about his family. And his gut feel is 'Go for it!'. If you have a similar, essentially positive reaction and feel energised (despite a few reasonable concerns), it's time to move on to the next stage. Prepare for take-off!

By contrast, if you have a strong negative reaction to any of the above three questions, you are experiencing what I call incongruence. Incongruence is when you know there is something wrong, but can't put your finger on what exactly, or why, or how serious the objection actually is, or . . . some part of you is uncomfortable about making that decision and you do not necessarily know why that is. Leap ahead to the troubleshooting guide.

↗ **brilliant** recap

Use the decision simulator to ask yourself eight questions:

1 What is the decision I face?

2 So, what am I going to do?

3 What do I want to happen?

- Move towards positive outcomes, not away from problems.

4 How will I know when it has happened?

- What specifically will I *see* when I have this goal?

- What specifically will I *hear* when I have this goal?

- What specifically will I *feel* when I have this goal?

5 Why is the decision important to me?

- If I took that decision and it worked out, what would that do for me personally?

- Knowing that, what would that enable me to experience that is even more important or bigger?

6 What could go wrong? And what could I do about that?

- List four things that could go wrong.

- Sort out any irrational fears.

- For the rational fears, ask 'What am I going to do about this?'

7 What are the first three steps?

8 Where have I got to now?

- Does it seem right at three levels: head, heart and gut?

- If it does seem right – don't rush into action. It's time to plan the decision: move on to Stage 2.

- If it doesn't seem right, consider why. Go to the troubleshooting guide.

CHAPTER 4

Stage 2: Prepare for the decision

The simulator should have given you a good overall sense of the decision you face. Now the more detailed work must begin. This chapter is about doing the preparation necessary to make a brilliant decision.

Some models of decision making present it as a neat linear process. First you establish your outcomes. Then you gather information. Done that? Good, so now it's time to create some options. Then you must evaluate these options. Then you have to decide ... Brilliant decision making is rather more subtle than this.

Begin by getting the basic time issues sorted out. How long do you have to make the decision? I have included a few tips and tricks on how to buy some extra time if you are under pressure.

After that, you enter a kind of cycle. You start gathering information. You soon become aware of options, which usually send you off in search of more information. This search may or may not change the options. The more you learn, the more some options become 'runners' and others drop out of view. Finally, you are ready to make the central decision.

All the way through this process you will be thinking. You will have some sessions of conscious thinking, for example sitting down with a piece of paper and listing pros and cons of an option. And underneath it all, that amazing super-computer called your unconscious mind will be working away at the problem.

To simplify my explanation, I have broken down the component parts of this cycle into separate sections – but please don't infer from this that they actually follow each other, one neatly after the other, as they do on the page. They actually interweave and build up to your readiness to decide – a bit like a piece of music in which instruments come and go but which slowly builds up to a crescendo.

Understand and take control of how much time you have

The first piece of information you need about a decision is: 'How long have I got?'

This may be a deadline you set yourself, as part of the SMART goal-setting process, or it may be imposed on you by someone else.

> you very often have more time to complete a decision than you think

When someone else attempts to impose a decision on you it is extremely important to understand that you very often have more time to complete a decision than you think – or than other interested parties will tell you (their agenda is usually to get the decision they want as quickly as possible). Even when a deadline is imposed by another party and appears to be fixed, you can often buy time, using one or some of the strategies that I shall outline below.

When I coach people who have become very stressed about a decision they are facing, the point about their having more time than they think is the first one I make to them. Their reaction is almost always one of intense relief – sometimes accompanied by incredulity. 'But I've been given an ultimatum . . .'

It is extremely important to make big decisions in a way that ensures you are in control of your own decision-making process and that you feel as relaxed as possible. Dodgy salespeople know this, which is why they always 'inject scarcity' into a situation: 'Today, for one day only . . .' By contrast:

'Deals always get better. Say "No" until your tongue bleeds!!!'
Harvey MacKay, American business author

Below I present some strategies for buying yourself time and the accompanying 'emotional space' to help you make a brilliant decision. Of course, the time you buy has to be used well – don't just use the bought time to avoid the decision. (This is the ostrich approach: 'Phew, that nasty decision has gone away, for a bit anyway. I can now forget all about it and get on with my nice, ordinary life . . .')

Ask for more time

By far the easiest way to create extra time to make a decision is simply to ask for it, politely.

The way I buy myself more time without offending anyone is by making a statement along the following lines:

That's a really exciting opportunity and thank you for offering it to me. However, I'm the kind of person who finds it difficult and uncomfortable to make decisions on the spot. Therefore, I'd really appreciate if you would let me do what fits in best with the way I work and how I feel. Give me a little time to go away and reflect on this. I'll give you my answer very soon. I genuinely see your offer as very valuable; this is simply the way that I operate.

You're being honest here – the offer is interesting but you need time. If you explain that the way you make decisions is that you require time to think and that they would be doing you a huge disservice by pressurising you to make a decision straight away, most people would reply: 'OK. If that's how you decide, then I have to respect it.'

If someone is unwilling to respect the way you make decisions, then it is also questionable whether this is somebody you wish to have many dealings with. Arguably this time-buying strategy has a secondary role, of seeing if the people you are dealing with respond in a fair-minded way. Just as you usually have more time than you think you do, there are usually more options than you think you have. If you are unhappy with the person with whom you are dealing – walk away. As far as the law is concerned, once you hit 18, as long as you don't commit a criminal offence, you don't have to say 'Yes' to anything!

 **brilliant** tip

> If you are unhappy with the person with whom you are dealing – walk away.

Say you need to do something else

Specify something you have to do before you can decide. This is the classic 'I'll have to discuss this with my wife/ husband/parents/friend/landlord etc.' line. It's classic because it works.

It's best used with integrity – when there really is only one thing you need to do before you decide, and that is speak to x. You will get pursued from then on – 'Spoken to x yet?'

Use a conditional yes

The above can be supported by a 'conditional yes', if you feel the need. This is a reply along the lines of: 'That's an amazing offer, and my instinct is to say "Yes". However . . .' Then add the condition, like 'I need to check with other people/think it through a bit before I can confirm'.

People sometimes use this as a pure time-buying technique – in other words they don't mean the 'Yes' at all. I leave it up to you to decide if you want to go down that route. I would say that even though such practice is not hugely ethical, it is not as annoying as the person who says 'Yes' with great sincerity and then, with equal sincerity, changes their mind, probably several times. And also that it should only be used dishonestly if someone is putting undue pressure on you. In such a case, they aren't playing straight either, and you have a moral right to protect yourself from such pressure. It can be the only alternative to screaming 'No!' at someone and storming out (more about saying 'No' later . . .).

Create a smokescreen

Another way of buying time is to create what I call a smokescreen. Basically, you just talk – at great length, about all the various issues you face and concerns that you have and the questions you need to ask and . . . You may even drift on to a different topic while you are talking. After a while, the other person will become sufficiently irritated to want to bring the encounter to a close: their desire to get an instant decision out of you has been exceeded by their desire to get you to shut up.

When you notice this, ask them if you can let them know next week (specify a date). At this point, the person will probably agree. They aren't enjoying the conversation, and by offering an outcome at a future date, you have satisfied their ego that they have got some kind of commitment out of you.

You can refine this by building a condition of the kind suggested above into the outcome: 'I'll have a chat with x first . . .'. On the date agreed, you can then send them an e-mail or a text message – no need to talk – saying that you haven't been able to get hold of x yet, but you will let them know once you have managed to catch up with x.

Gather information

Now you can start to gather information. Begin with a *brainstorm*. Write down everything you need to find out, where you think you can do this, and everyone you need to sound out. Then make some kind of *plan* of how you will get hold of all this information and when.

There are essentially two types of information you need to gather. First is factual stuff; the second is about how key people might react to your decision.

Factual information

In my view, books remain the single best source of information. The words 'author' and 'authority' come from the same root: a good book is the condensed wisdom of someone who really knows their stuff, and has worked with a team of experts on communicating that clearly to produce the best possible guide they can. For any author worth their salt, a book is how they nail their colours to the mast: 'This is what I know, and I'm prepared to tell the world that is the case.' Most authors are happy to be contacted by readers: as I've said, my e-mail is robbie@nlpschool.com – please use it if you have a question or a comment for me; I'd be delighted to hear from you.

'Are you reading the books that will take you to where you want to go in the next five to ten years time? Excellent question!'
Jim Rohn, American writer and motivational speaker

Use the power of the internet, too. Relying on a single internet source is not recommended – even the wonderful Wikipedia gets the odd nutter on there who plants misinformation. But as a part of your information hunt, it's marvellous.

And talk to people!

Close friends know you and (usually) wish you well – though remember that they do have agendas for you (a topic I shall discuss later).

Other people will have specialist knowledge. Such people can be easier to access than you think. Through friends or friends of friends, you can get hold of almost anyone ('Six degrees of separation' stand between us and anyone else on earth, if the play of that title is to be believed.) Experts will usually respond well to a simple e-mail or telephone message stating who you are, your connection to the person they know and that you'd like ten minutes of their time to discuss whatever issue it is. If you are not selling anything and your situation is simply that you want to gain some knowledge, many people will be glad to offer a little help.

Coaches and mentors

These people are not so much providers of specific information as guides to help you along the journey of your decision.

If you have time and money, hire a *coach*. It's best to hire a professional rather than get an amateur: you need professionalism here. Serious coaches will often offer reduced rates to members of the public paying with their own money (much of their work is corporate), so ask.

Coaches will draw from you thoughts, ideas, feelings, values and wants that you were hardly aware of but which will have a bearing on your decision. They will create a 'safe space' for you to discuss options – to plunge into an idea then suddenly change your mind with no loss of face. Coaches have no agenda for their clients, unlike friends, family or colleagues, who usually want you to stay as you are.

(Some coaches have an agenda of getting results. They like it best when they work with a client on an issue and the client then takes action on that issue. However, sometimes the best thing to do is to do nothing – don't be railroaded into acting by an over-eager coach.)

Can you get a *mentor* for your decision making? The best mentors are not the ones who provide specific advice, but those who instil the right attitudes in you: the right beliefs and values, not just skills.

I had a wonderful mentor for decision making: my father. He sometimes gave me specific advice but other times just said it was 'up to me'. What he always did was give me confidence that I should go out there, make a decision and follow it through, and that if things went wrong, I could make new decisions and get back on track again, better informed. He was a courageous, sparky man, and he managed to instil some of these qualities in me, for which I am hugely grateful.

Other people are less fortunate in their family. If that includes you, you can find a mentor elsewhere.

---

brilliant example

Anna rowed with both her parents, who lived in a small town and seemed obsessed by 'what the neighbours think'. She moved up to London straight from school, and got a job in a clothes shop. Lucy was a customer at the shop, and she and Anna got talking about their mutual interest in fashion: they became friends, despite Lucy being ten years older. Lucy runs her own design business, and when she needed an assistant, took Anna on. She became a mentor for Anna, happy to talk through any topic and keen to encourage her to follow her own passions. Even when Anna decided she wanted to leave the business, Lucy wished her well and they remain in contact.

The best way to find a mentor is simply to look around, find someone you consider experienced and helpful, and then ask him or her. The last part is usually the most difficult, but people are often surprisingly flattered to be asked and take it as a compliment.

Sounding out significant others

Having key people behind a decision is a major factor in how well it works, so you need to know as soon as possible who will be rooting for you and who will be in your way. I always sound people out (very tactfully) as soon as I can.

If a subject is very touchy, you can try a more indirect approach. For example, Jenny is in a relationship with Paul, but it is not a happy one. She is thinking of leaving him, but fears he might get violent if she does. She could try talking about another relationship, and seeing what his response is. 'You know Clara. She and Bill aren't happy. What do you think Bill might do if Clara leaves?' If Paul clenches his fist and says 'make her bloody well regret it', it's time to plan not just a departure but an escape. I will look at Clara's progress with this decision again later in the book.

brilliant example

I was in a pub with a friend meeting his new girlfriend. She related to me – with great glee – a story of what happened when her boss fired her: she bought a catering jar of mustard and went to the office that night and poured the contents into every computer, printer and filing cabinet. 'That showed him!' she said proudly. I watched the horror spread over my friend's face ... But at least he now knew what to expect if he decided to end the relationship (or rather, what to expect, now that he had decided to end the relationship).

'Either flatter or crush your enemies, but never leave anyone in a position where they can take revenge.'

Machiavelli, Italian political philosopher

Luckily most people in most decisions won't be as extreme as Machiavelli – but you will probably encounter some opposition. Good: you now know that. It's time to get working on persuading them round to your point of view. This is a topic I shall discuss in Chapter 6 on implementation – after all, you've not made the decision yet.

Create and evaluate options (the cycle)

Options tend to *crystallise* rather than just appear all neat and tidy. They start as rough ideas, and gradually firm up into practicable courses of action as you research and think.

If you are stuck for options, try brainstorming again: 'All the things I could do'.

Generating options will create the need for further research. A kind of cycle is set up. You think of a new option; you go away and find out what it actually entails in practice; this makes you aware of a further option, which needs further research (and so on). What you are effectively doing here is doing a rough plan of how you will implement your decision.

brilliant example

Nigel's mother is suffering from Alzheimer's. He must decide soon if she should go into a home. When? Which home? How will he find the money? Looking at options means thinking ahead.

You can *evaluate* options in all sorts of ways. Some people like to do intricate analyses of the good and bad points of every option. Others work through the list of options and pick out the best points of each, to create a 'must have' list. Others do no conscious thought at all, but let their unconscious mind set to work, filling it with ideas and finding out which ones, after a period of reflection, 'feel right'.

Find the style of evaluation that suits you.

At this point, you do not need to come up with one 'right' decision, but a couple or (or maybe three) front runners, which you can take to the next stage, where you actually make up your mind.

> you do not need to come up with one 'right' decision

Before heading there, I'd like to say a little about that most valuable and useful thing – confusion.

Be confused!

One thing that many people hate about decision making is the sense of confusion that can overcome them when they are going through this cycle of crystallising options, finding out more information and generally mulling stuff over. This can be particularly unpleasant for people who have swallowed the myth of 'decisiveness', and who think they are being indecisive and weak and generally making a mess of everything.

Actually, confusion is a very good thing.

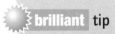 **brilliant** tip

Confusion is an essential stage in the making of a good decision.

Confusion means that change is taking place. New information is sinking in; new ways of fitting all our information together are forming. If we aren't confused on the way to a big decision, the decision probably won't move us very far forward.

'Gentlemen, I take it we are all in complete agreement here . . . Then I propose we postpone further discussion until our next meeting, to

*give ourselves time to develop disagreement and perhaps gain some
understanding of what the decision is all about.'*

Alfred P. Sloan, Chairman of General Motors at its height

The Change House is a useful and popular model. It was originally created by Swedish psychologist Claes Janssen as the Four
Rooms of Change, but has since been modified by various
thinkers – it is the modified, and best known form that I shall
use. The model shows clearly both the overall importance and
the specific role of confusion in the decision process.

When life is going well, we are in the Room of Contentment.
There are no pressing decisions we need to make. In fact, it gets
so comfortable that we go and sit on the Sun Deck, stretch out
on a sun lounger and have our favourite cold drink.

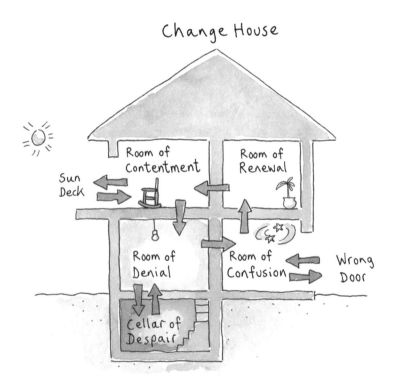

But life, as it tends to do, continues, and problems start to emerge. Gradually, we sink from our Room of Contentment to the Room of Denial. This strange room looks exactly like the Room of Contentment, but it feels totally different, as if a ghost had entered the Room of Contentment and frozen its warm sunny atmosphere. Things have gone wrong but we are pretending everything is still fine. Things get worse. We may actually sink further, into the Cellar of Despair.

Finally, however, we make the decision that we need to do something, even though we don't know what it is.

We move into the Room of Confusion. Here we are having all sorts of ideas, talking to people and having thoughts, though we're still not sure what to do. Sometimes we come up with a decision, walk out of a door, put the plan in action and realise it doesn't work – Wrong Door. We scurry back into the Room of Confusion. Better to be back in that room than to have stuck with the Wrong Door decision. (A key theme of this book, as you will find out, is that mistakes are healthy – as the NLP saying has it: there is no such thing as failure, only feedback.) However, we don't want to stay in the Room of Confusion forever.

> there is no such thing as failure, only feedback

Eventually, we will formulate and make a decision that will take us up to the Room of Renewal. Here, we find the decision brings us all sorts of unexpected good things. We are full of energy and have all sorts of positive ideas; suddenly our life is turning around – it's as if we've been reborn.

After a while, this enthusiasm begins to wane and we find ourselves back in the Room of Contentment. Once we have spent some time there, we go and sit on the Sun Deck – but we know what will happen eventually!

'*The ability to tolerate confusion is a sign of genius.*'
                    Albert Einstein, mathematical physicist

Allow yourself to be confused. In NLP if someone says to you, 'I'm confused', the response is 'Excellent!'

I want to conclude this section with a comment on the opposite of confusion: certainty. We all like to be certain about things. I'm certain about the material in this book: I've used it for years; it works. But at the same time, a desire for total certainty about everything can be damaging.

Arguably the only thing that is certain in life is change. I think that most people believe that if they work hard, do the right things and have a little luck, life will work out for them. In reality, everything changes, and if we do not keep up with those changes – in our selves and in the world around us – we risk our goals and ambitions slipping from our grasp.

If people become too attached to a full set of ideas, it can cut them off from any change. Not only will they be unwilling to change, but they will filter all the information that comes into them in the light of whatever set of beliefs they hold. This will mean that in a time of rapid change their information becomes ever less accurate. A vicious circle can result. As their understanding of the world gets narrower and narrower, that world begins to look ever more frightening. This fear makes them cling all the harder to their core belief – which makes them filter incoming information about change all the more ruthlessly. And so on. In the Change House model, these people sit in the Room of Denial, then end up in the Cellar of Despair (or, its neighbour, the Utility Room of Whistling in the Dark) – until the entire house suddenly collapses, thanks to the termites that have been noisily undermining it for ages.

 **tip**

'Believing is seeing.' Think about it ...

By contrast, some people follow change like sheep, ever spouting the latest fashionable idea, or sporting the latest fashion item, even if it doesn't suit them at all. The stereotype 'middle-aged trendy' trying to 'make it with the kids on the street' quite rightly invites derision (William Hague, a serious, thoughtful but rather middle-aged Conservative politician, should never have been photographed in a baseball cap at the Notting Hill Carnival!).

Brilliant decision making allows us to deal with change on *our* terms.

 **recap**

Prepare for the central decision:

1   Understand and take control of how much time you have. Tips and tricks to gain extra time:

   ● Ask for it.

   ● Specify something you have to do before you can decide.

   ● The conditional yes.

   ● Use a smokescreen as an escape route.

2   Gather information – from books, the internet, talking to people, etc.:

   ● Learn more facts.

   ● Get coaching and mentoring.

   ● Sound out significant others.

3   Create and evaluate options. Enter a cycle of gathering information, thinking and considering what to do:

   ● Work towards some front runners.

   ● Balance conscious and unconscious mind-work.

4   Be confused – take some time to *not* know what to do:

   ● The Change House model teaches us that confusion is a natural part of the change process.

CHAPTER 5

Stage 3: Make the decision

You've done your research, come up with options, researched them more, done a lot of thinking, got pretty confused. Out of this, a clear picture will ultimately develop. This is often of two options – it could be 'do something or don't do it'; it could be two different courses of action.

Then you decide. How, exactly, do you do this?

The moment of decision

The honest answer is that you don't actually 'do' anything. If you've done the basics in the previous chapters, a proper decision will simply emerge from the process, as your unconscious mind works its way to a decision.

The actual way in which the decision then *reveals* itself to the conscious mind varies from person to person.

---

brilliant examples

- Sheila maintained a great level of health. She explained that she just knew when she was beginning to get run down and did something about it. I asked questions to drill down to the precise moment when she decided to arrange more exercise. She explained, while gesturing with one hand, that she had a picture of herself lying in bed and a feeling of heaviness. Gesturing with the other hand, she said she then had a picture of herself walking down a city street with a yoga mat under her arm and felt light and full of energy. 'When I have those two pictures, I say to myself I want that one (the yoga mat), not that one (the bed), and then I go and start booking some events for the following week.'

- Stuart, an entrepreneur, says, 'I usually end up with two options. I think one, then the other, then one, then the other – then finally one of these triumphs. I know what to do.'

- 'I hear a voice in my head,' says Tracy, a life coach. 'I know that sounds a bit strange, but that's what happens. It tells me, "That's the thing to do. Now get on with it!".'

- 'I give the various options colours,' says Max, who's a graphic designer. 'After a while, I see the colour of the best option in my mind. It just stays there, and that tells me it's the winner.'

- Here's Winston Churchill, the day he became Prime Minister:

'I was conscious of a profound sense of relief: at last I had the authority to give directions over the whole scene. I felt as if I were walking with destiny and all my past life had been but a preparation for this hour and for this trial … I thought I knew a good deal about it all and I was sure I should not fail.'

What all the examples above have in common is that they represent moments of what I call *congruence*. I've already talked about incongruence – well, here's its very welcome opposite. It means that we know what we have to do. The decision is wholehearted; we believe deeply in its rightness and necessity. (Note that it does not necessarily mean we are 'joyous' about the decision: it might mean leaving a partner or dismissing someone from a job, or some other difficult and painful action. But we know it is the right thing to do.)

The examples above all deliver the same message, but they do so in very different ways. How do you tell yourself that you have decided in this congruent way? Try this exercise.

Checking congruence

Like the meditation and visualisations earlier in the book, this is best listened to. Get a friend to read it to you, record yourself or visit www.brilliantdecisionmaking.com for a free MP3 download.

First, look inside for how you spot a congruent decision:

When you have made a major decision at some point in the past, you may recall that although it seemed a bit frightening, nonetheless you knew it was the right thing to do – bring back a memory of what it was like just before you made that type of decision. Have you remembered a specific time? Where were you in a room? Outdoors? Was someone else with you? Any important decision will do. Got it? Have you thought of one like that right now? OK, notice your head, heart and gut at that time back then. For many people, it is not always an entirely positive feeling; just bring to mind what was happening to you just before you made that decision. Perhaps at that time the decision which you faced was challenging – were some other people affected? You may have been concerned about that decision – perhaps there were some risks involved – yet, at the time when you made that decision, although you had no idea what was going to happen, there was some part of you that really wanted to go with this, that knew it was the right thing to do. Although the consequences might be significant, you knew you were going to do it. Now bring that memory fully to your mind. Some people remember any words they said to themselves, others remember the pictures of the event, while others recall sounds or feelings. However you remember that memory, right now, is entirely correct; just allow yourself to fully regain that memory right now, so you can re-experience that sensation leading up to a decision, right now. Have you got it? Do you know what it is like to have that sensation again, right now? Knowing that you are persuaded to take that course of action? Allow yourself to remember this sensation for the next section. You have now created your congruent decision reference memory. Spend a few moments repeating this material so you can easily access that memory for future use.

You might choose to contrast this with how you know you are unhappy with a decision, or not ready to decide.

Likewise, think of a time in the past when you were just about to make a major decision, or were pressed by someone else to make one, that you somehow knew was not right and you simply didn't want to do it. Often people notice a sensation in their body, or words, or pictures that seem somehow ominous. Some people report a 'numb' sensation, as if they were no longer really there. Every person has a unique experience of this kind: allow yourself to think of a time like that when you had that sensation. Often the feeling is not at all pleasant, with a sense of intensity and pressure. Other times, there is some kind of powerful conflict with one part of you wanting to do it and another very concerned. Often when we make decisions in this kind of state, we know we are in denial of these internal warnings, and that sense of knowing that and still pressing ahead adds further to this sense. Bring back a memory of what it was like just before you made that type of decision. Have you remembered a specific time? Where were you? In a room? Outdoors? Was someone else with you? Any important decision will do. Got it? Have you thought of one like that right now? OK, notice your head, heart and gut at that time back then. Although at that time in the past you did not know what was going to happen, you knew that you didn't want to do it. Once again, with that decision that seemed wrong at the time, find out what the pictures, sounds, feelings and things you may have been saying to yourself at the time were like. You are now experiencing what I call incongruence about a decision. You know there is something wrong, but can't put your finger on what exactly, or why, or how serious the objection actually is, or ... Some part of you is really uncomfortable about making that decision and you do not necessarily know why that is. You know the *difference from the nervous and excited feeling of making a decision you want to make. Notice what some people call a feeling of dread. Got it? Allow yourself to remember this sensation for the next section. You have now created your incongruence reference memory. Spend a few moments repeating this material so you can easily access that memory for future use.*

Please note that this process of knowing when you feel congruent about a decision is not a crystal ball: it doesn't guarantee that the decision will turn out to be magically successful, only that it is the best decision you can make, given what you know about yourself, the people around you and the facts of the situation. What it does tell you is that:

- The decision has a good chance of working out.
- If it does go all wrong, then you will be at peace with yourself.

If you make a decision which felt congruent but which doesn't work out, you tend to accept it as a lesson in life. If you make a decision which is incongruent, and things go wrong, that's when you feel you have shot yourself in the foot and recriminations, sadness and anger can creep in.

In practice, few decisions go totally 'wrong'. Almost any decision is better than none. Even ones that appear not to work out as planned produce change and the opportunity to learn and grow – especially if the decision was made wholeheartedly at the time.

 **brilliant** tip

Know when you know you've made a genuine, wholehearted decision, and when you know you are about to do the opposite.

Here are some other hints to set yourself up to make brilliant decisions.

Get in the right state

An impending decision can often feel threatening, and it's easy to get the adrenaline pumping and for the mind to get into 'fight, flight or freeze' mode. This is a very helpful reaction in certain situations, but not for making good decisions.

Yet it is often when we are most hyper that we make decisions: some people who find decision making difficult actually wait until they are in a highly emotional state to decide, as decision making seems easy then. And it is easy – but the decisions will be poor quality. If you were deciding on buying a house, would you wait till you were very angry about something to make the decision?

The main problem with highly emotional states is that we often do not realise we are in them until they are over. It is a key life skill to understand our own moods and to rise above them, and say, 'I'm in such and such a mood now; I won't make a decision now, but later, when I am calmer'.

brilliant tip

When you are dealing with highly emotional matters:

- stop
- notice the state you are in
- wait until you calm down.

It's also true that a happy mind makes better decisions than an unhappy one. This can be a 'Catch 22' situation, where you are damned if you do and damned if don't – for example, if you feel depressed and need to make decisions to lift yourself out of depression but can't make decisions because you're depressed. Can you at least get away to a place that you associate with happiness, and let your mind do the deciding there,

> a happy mind makes better decisions than an unhappy one

rather than stay where you are now, in a place where you feel under pressure? Can you spend some time in the company of someone whom you like, and do fun things with them? Lift your mood. Not with alcohol or drugs: the mood-lifting has to be genuine, not chemically induced.

A particularly bad state in which to make a decision is one where you have given yourself a kind of inner ultimatum, along the lines of: 'I won't be happy until I have made this decision.' This is a trap! You will not make a good decision in this frame of mind. Instead, can you be happy right now, then make the decision? The first 'ennobling truth' in Buddhism is that 'Anguish is caused by wanting what you don't have, not by not having what you don't have'. Stop wanting so badly!

brilliant tip

If we want something in our life, it is usually because we want a specific feeling when we have got it. Why not just get that feeling in the first place?

Visualise your goals

Remember to use the visualisations used in the decision simulator (see pages 33–35) to focus your mind on your goals, which are what the decision is all about.

Sleep on it

Psychologists are still trying to fathom out exactly what the brain does while we sleep – but it certainly works away at problems, in my view all the more effectively because there's no 'noise' from our conscious daytime activity to put it off. I've lost count of the number of decisions that have become crystal clear after a night's sleep.

If you haven't got time to sleep on a decision then do something that is physical and which requires a measure of concentration, so your conscious mind is taken off the problem.

Done all those? If you are truly wholehearted and congruent about your decision, I recommend a brief 'last walk through it' before making that big internal commitment. Go quickly through the following to recall the steps so far:

- The decision simulator – recall what came up.
- The planning phase – remember your plans.
- The people issues – remember what conversations you may need to have shortly.
- Compare your state to your congruent and incongruent reference memories.
- Come to the moment of decision.
- Decide!

I often like to take a long walk and have a final think about things while I go through this process.

And then it is done. Decision made! You can put this book away now . . .

No!

You have not stopped deciding, simply moved the decision-making process on to its next stage. There is still some way to go – as there was for Churchill, who had a number of implementation issues to deal with, such as winning the Second World War . . .

But when you do reach this state of congruent decision, give yourself a treat for having done so. Well done!

If you are not congruent, of course, then it's time to find out why. Some part of you is not happy with the decision. Which part? Why? What can you do about it? Go to the troubleshooting guide on page 101.

If you've done all the troubleshooting you can and you still feel unconvinced in some way, you can delay the decision. (If you have a time limit, you may have to decline: the time is not right for you, and that's just how it is.)

Not acting can be a brilliant decision if the action is not right for you.

▶ brilliant example

I was once coaching someone who was recently divorced. He told me he wanted to settle down with someone again. Obviously if he wanted coaching on the subject, he had sensed something was wrong with this potential decision. I asked him to list all the benefits of a single life that he enjoyed, and finally he said, 'I don't want to settle down now; I want to stay single!'

He had decided *not* to act.

As an entrepreneur I'm probably a bit of a 'make it happen' sort of person. My solicitor often advises me: 'Robert, sometimes the best thing to do, and the hardest thing to, is to do nothing!'

Sometimes our unconscious mind knows it is best to wait a bit longer and see what shows up. This is very different to the kind of conflicts we deal with in the troubleshooting guide.

Live with it

Actually, my advice for what to do next – after celebrating – is nothing. For a short while, anyway. However right you feel your decision to be, it is wise to live with it for a bit before you leap into action.

Some people take what I call the kamikaze approach to decisions. The moment they have decided, they 'burn their bridges' – they go round telling everyone what they have decided, sign all the relevant documents (and so on).

This is often done by people who know they have a history of putting off or reversing decisions. OK: it is probably better than backsliding yet again. But much, much better is to master the art of brilliant decision making and decide in a way that gives you options and control.

decide in a way that
gives you options and
control

Another motive for bridge burning is a fear, among people who are normally pretty good at decision making, that for some reason there will be unusual pressure on them in this case to reverse this decision. In Greek mythology, Ulysses tied himself to the mast of his ship to avoid being seduced by the Sirens who lured sailors on to rocks. More recently, in 1989 the unification of Germany was rushed through by Chancellor Helmut Kohl at great expense, just in case the Soviet Union changed its mind about letting East Germany out of its grasp. People criticised Kohl for this – until a coup in 1991 threatened to put hard-line Communists back in power in the Kremlin, at which point Kohl's actions looked wise.

But as a rule, you don't have to do this.

brilliant tip

Give yourself a little time between deciding and acting. Enjoy this time. You'll probably find yourself full of plans – stay with them; start planning (but don't be wedded to any of them). Trust your unconscious mind to be mulling over the decision; if there is something really important you need to attend to, it will come to the surface and you can consult the troubleshooting guide.

Of course, you must leave this rather pleasant land of limbo after a while and start implementing. As a rule of thumb, I think a significant decision should be acted upon after about a week's living with it. But use your intuition: I once waited six weeks to implement a decision and, although I didn't change my mind, my ideas of how I was going to implement it kept improving. When the moment came when I had to put my cards on the table, I handled it all much better than I would have done if I had only waited a week.

You may have to pluck up a bit of courage to actually get things moving. Remind yourself of the nice feeling of congruence: you know this is right. (If you need reminders of this feeling, which you can access any time, make sure you have them – see page 65.)

brilliant example

Kate made the decision to buy a flat, then went away and 'lived with' that decision during a weekend at a music festival. She bought records of the artists performing there, and now plays these to remind her of that congruent feeling of 'Yes, I'm going to do it!'

Think of the outcomes towards which the decision is impelling you. And trust your decision-making skill. The next chapter is full of tips and tricks on how to overcome all those difficult things like saying 'No' to people, and dealing with any sudden hankerings after the old world you are leaving behind.

Check, of course, that you still believe that the decision is the right one – truly, congruently. Yes?

If the answer has become 'No', go to the troubleshooting guide.

But if it's still 'Yes', and it almost always is at this stage, then it's time to move on to the next phase – actually making it happen.

 **recap**

Make the central decision:

1   The moment of decision:

- Find out, from your past, your unique way of knowing when you have made a wholehearted or congruent decision. Also find out from your past how you know when you are not sure something is right (incongruence).

- Get yourself into the best possible state to make the decision.

- Decide.

- Notice if your experience of this decision fits with your unique way of knowing if a decision is congruent or incongruent.

- Congruent? Move on.

- Incongruent? Why? Think it through further. Consult the troubleshooting guide.

2   Live with it:

- If you have decided, live with the decision for a while before you commit yourself.

- Still congruent? (Probably you will be.) Time to continue on to the next chapter.

- Not sure again? Head for the troubleshooting guide.

CHAPTER 6

Stage 4: Put the decision into practice – make it happen!

Once you make the big, central decision, you have to put it into practice. Or 'implement' it, to use the jargon.

Many well-researched, congruently made decisions can go wrong here: this stage is hugely important. There is no point in going through the pain and effort of planning and making a decision, and then botching the way you make it happen.

A brilliant decision is not a kind of steamroller that you just jump on to, start, then drive in a dead straight line thereafter. Brilliant decisions are implemented artfully. The post-decision world will not be as you thought it would be, because however well you mapped that world out you will have missed something, and because the making of your decision will of itself change things. So you adapt to that – with more decisions.

Yes, sometimes this means emulating the steamroller and forging on past (or over) various nay-sayers and other obstacles. But more often it means adapting. In extreme cases, it means reversing the decision altogether – which might seem a disaster, but is almost always actually just another form of progress: you don't end up back at the same place.

NLP trainer Stephen Gilligan tells the story of a famous fencer who was once asked the secret of fencing. He said that it lay in holding the sword like a bird in one's hand, neither too tight nor

too loose. If you hold the bird too tight, you can crush it. If you hold it too loose, it can wriggle free and fly away.

Ask yourself if you are holding the decision too tight or too loose. This metaphor will help your unconscious mind tell you where the right course of action lies.

Let's look at some basic aspects of making it happen.

Plan your implementation

Rather boringly, the first thing to do is to plan. This needs to be done with some precision: the skills you need here are those of the project manager – an eye for detail, the ability to schedule events, a determination to stick to a timetable and make things happen.

Project managers make a distinction between *exclusive* and *concurrent tasks*. Exclusive tasks can't be done at the same time: you have to finish x before you can start y. For example, you can't start renovating a property until you have signed all the legal documents that ensure it is yours. Concurrent tasks can be done at the same time: you can have someone in fixing the roof, a plumber in sorting the bathroom, and get to work yourself on the garden (just make sure you've got a good supply of coffee . . .).

Project managers also give themselves clear *milestones*, times by which certain tasks need to be done. As with all brilliant decision making, there needs to be some flexibility in these – but not too much. We're back with the fencer and the bird again.

Jenny, whom we met earlier, has definitely decided she is going to leave Paul. She lived with the decision for a week – any doubts disappeared last night when she dropped a plate and he yelled at her that she was a stupid cow. (Even then, her mother's voice piped up in her head that she'd been called worse things, and that Paul was very charming sometimes, especially when he stays off the drink . . .).

Jenny makes a list of things she needs to do:

- The big one: tell him it's over.
- Find somewhere to go to straight away.
- Find somewhere to live long term.
- Tell her friends and family.
- Move her possessions away from their flat and across to her new, temporary place.

These, of course, need going into in greater depth. 'Tell him it's over' isn't just a simple task. What would be the best time and place to do this? (Even though Paul didn't come up with anything too scary when Jenny ran the 'Bill and Clara' story past him, she's still a little afraid he might get violent; maybe a public place would be better than at home.) She should plan what she's going to say, and practise that beforehand with a friend. It would be good to have a friend waiting by a phone to talk to immediately afterwards, or even waiting outside wherever she decides she will break the news. Can she do anything to lessen the blow for him? (Probably not, but have a think about it.) Naturally, she's afraid of going through with this – what can she do to get her courage up just before she 'goes into bat'? (I'll present an exercise later.)

Going into this level of detail will also throw up more 'to dos' to add to the list.

Some of you may think Jenny's approach a bit clinical, but it's really just common sense. The alternative is coming out with stuff at the wrong time, or ending up doing something meaner like dumping Paul by text or a letter – or, worst of all, perpetually delaying telling him 'till the time feels right' and ending up still with him in a year's time.

Deal with the people issues

This usually breaks down into two main topics:

● Influencing: getting other individuals or groups to buy in to your decision.

● Insisting: saying 'No', or insisting on your decision when people refuse to accept it.

I'll look at these in turn.

Influencing: getting others to buy in

Often, you will need to recruit some people to help you make the decision work – either as active participants, like Jenny's friend in the example above, or simply by accepting the changes your decision will bring about.

> the best way to bring people round to your view is gently and subtly

The best way to bring people round to your view is gently and subtly. People are often more shocked by the thought of change – any change – than by the actual changes planned. So sow the seeds of change in someone's mind, then let their own unconscious work on it.

Recently I wanted to go away on a brief holiday on my own. I first mentioned it to my wife in passing and she seemed slightly irritated. I didn't make a big deal about it. I then mentioned it again the next day and said I wanted to book the flight; she seemed perfectly happy and suggested I use our frequent flyer scheme!

I also use this technique in business. I will tell my colleagues something like, 'I've been thinking it would be a good idea to explore a few options. Here are my ideas . . . Have a think about these, and let's talk about them later.'

brilliant tip

When you present other people with change, it is important for you to allow them the time to sleep on it and to think it over. Often a hostile initial reaction can be later met with agreement. A key part of the art of influencing is to know how to be patient and give people time to come around.

Choose your moment to talk to the person you want to influence – the moment that suits them. When are they most relaxed? Many an attempt at influencing has failed because the influencer chose a bad moment to announce a new plan.

brilliant example

Three Japanese shoguns were looking at a song bird in a tree. Each was asked what they would do if the bird did not sing. One of them said, 'Make it!' Another said, 'Kill it!' A third one simply said 'Wait'.

The first two didn't last. The third one unified Japan under the Samurai system and his family ruled for ten generations.

If you are setting up a meeting with someone you want to influence:

● Make an appointment to see them at a time that suits them.

- Give them a hint in advance about what the meeting is about. If you don't do this, they will start imagining all sorts of things: for example their minds may be drawn back to sitting outside the headmaster's study at school. Such imaginings can create a mild resentment, and you do not want to start the meeting in that tone.

At this meeting, there will usually be a clash between two desirables – a clash that you have to make sense of, situation by situation.

- Desirable 1 is that you need to set the agenda. This encounter is about the changes *you* are making and what you want the person to do to help you with these. You must not let it get hijacked on to another topic.

- Desirable 2 is that the other person needs to 'state their truth'. If you just steamroller over them – 'This is what I'm doing; this is what I want you to do, OK?' – you will either not get their assent or you will get false assent (a rather grudging 'Yes' that does not actually get followed up in practice).

The art of letting someone speak from the heart but remaining in control of the overall agenda of the conversation is a considerable one, and well worth mastering.

The best advice I can give is to be reasonably upfront with your agenda, then consciously hand over to the other person: 'So what do you feel about that?' Really listen when they start replying. Deal with any specific objections. Can any win/win outcomes be negotiated? If there are issues that look like they aren't going to be sorted in that discussion, leave them for another one. Be respectful and listen carefully.

If you know the person, it can help hugely if you use words that they use and cite examples from their life. Everyone has a representation of reality in their mind, and if you can locate your decision in *their* representation rather than try and force your version of the world on to them, you will find acceptance much easier. You can also match them in other ways, such as posture or breathing pattern – as long as this is done subtly, and doesn't descend into mimicry. This is called 'pacing and leading' in NLP.

Sometimes, of course, influencing doesn't work. The person won't help you with your decision, and that's that. In that case, it is time to 'tell it as it is'.

Insisting

'If you can't say "No" to someone, then "Yes" has no value.'
Ed Hines, British martial arts and NLP teacher

Sometimes influencing is too soft a tool. If you decide to end a relationship, you normally have to go through a rather horrible scene with your soon-to-be-ex, where you say you are leaving. The same applies if you decide to dismiss an employee: you don't 'influence' them to leave, you tell them.

Insisting is often saying 'No' to someone. But sometimes, it's saying: 'Yes. Despite your disapproval, I'm going to do x.'

brilliant example

Naomi loved Karl, a man who came from a different religious faith to her, who she had been secretly dating for two years while at college. After graduation they moved in together and informed Naomi's parents, who had told her since childhood that she had to marry in her own faith. Naomi received a lot of pressure to give up her relationship with Karl. Tonight she was going to tell her parents of their plan to be married. She knew she would have to assert that although she understood their disappointment that he was not of their faith, she would like their blessing; nonetheless she would go ahead with the marriage whatever they said – Karl was her soulmate and her mind was made up.

Insisting is best done in person. A letter over which you have clearly taken a lot of thought is the next best substitute. I do not think getting a friend to do it or sending a brief text or e-mail are acceptable (unless the decision is a trivial one) – this is just plain cowardice!

More generally, there are two ways not to insist:

- The Rambo way: Shout at the person 'I'm doing x, and if you don't like it you can go to hell', then storm out of the room, slamming the door so hard that a picture dislodges itself from the wall.

- The Uriah Heep way: 'Oh, please say it's all right. I'll do anything to make it up to you if you'll let me do x . . .'

brilliant tips

If you want to insist in a way that is firm but respectful:

- Imagine there's an invisible shield between you and the person, that will deflect any negative energy that they may send towards you. (This may seem a bit hippy, but it works!)

- Own the decision. Say that this is your decision, not that 'I've been forced to do x'. Say also (if it's true) that it has been a tough decision to make.

- Be honest about the contents. Don't mince words and present a 'spun' half-strength version of what you are intending to do.

- Acknowledge the other person's feelings.

- Negotiate. Not like Uriah Heep, but adult-to-adult: 'Is there anything I can do to make it better for you?' The wise insister has anticipated the kind of replies they might get and will be in a position to say quickly if an option is possible. If you're not sure whether a concession is possible or not, buy time.

- Don't waver.

- Engineer an end. Egos will often get invested in such encounters, so don't focus on getting the last word. Just get out of there when it's time to go.

Practise insisting. Do it in front of a large mirror (look at *all* your body language and make it assertive – in other words, carrying conviction but not aggression). You can also role-play with a friend. If you are saying 'No' to someone, practise it: do a simple exercise where the friend asks 'Would you like to go to the cinema with me tomorrow?' and you say 'No' – it will get the 'no-saying' muscles active.

Plan what you are going to say, too. Don't end up reading off a script, but do go into the encounter with a clear idea of all the points you need to get across.

Here is a good exercise for getting your spirits up before the Big Scene.

Preparing yourself for a stressful encounter

Think of three qualities you would like to have, for example courage, compassion and a light touch. For courage, think of a time when you showed courage. It doesn't need to be a significant event, simply saying 'No' to a telesales person will do. Then relive that memory. Imagine you are back there; see the location; remember any objects. Was anyone else there? Remember any sounds and any feelings you had. Allow yourself to re-experience that memory fully, right now. Now find a way of remembering this feeling; sometimes pinching your fingers or recalling an image or song can do it.

Now do the same for the other two qualities.

At the end, bring all three qualities to mind and allow them to mix together to produce a new compound state – then off you go.

It's important to understand that a major decision, especially about your personal life, may well involve quite a lot of insisting – despite all the influencing you have been trying. Lots of people will have slotted you into their life playing a particular role, and the 'new you' may no longer be suited to those roles.

If you are given an ultimatum, of the 'abandon your decision or else ...' type, what should you do?

It may be that the reaction is a knee-jerk one, which the person may well regret the next morning. So don't escalate. Say you'll discuss it later and get away as soon as possible.

If possible, use the time-buying techniques outlined earlier. If you can, start negotiating with the person to find out what their problem is and if there is anything you can do to mitigate it.

Some ultimatums may unravel over longer periods of time. Many a disowned son or daughter has been let back into the family fold after the birth of a child. Don't make it impossible for the other side to climb down, much as you might wish to.

One thing *not* to do is to be made the 'bad guy' by the ultimatum-giver. People who give ultimatums often also say, 'You made me do this'. No. They chose to act in that way.

Deal with buyer's remorse

 brilliant definition

Buyer's remorse

A feeling, after you have acted on a decision, that you have made a mistake. It affects many people and is irrational: it is not linked to the quality of the decision (in other words, it is not the same as the sudden realisation of an actual mistake, it just feels like that). It almost always goes away after a short time, once you have become used to the changes that your decision has bought about.

The phenomenon is most common with decisions to purchase goods, hence the name, but it can occur with any decision.

I must admit that I do not suffer from buyer's remorse. Once I've made a decision and am implementing it, I get on with it. I don't find myself assailed by voices questioning whether I made a good decision after all. I've learnt to trust my decision-making process.

However, some people do find this a problem – apparently a lot of car advertising is aimed at soothing a buyer's remorse ('Yes, you *did* do the right thing in buying an X14: look, here's a guy wearing black tie with a gorgeous lady beside him driving one along an empty Highland road . . .') and these ads are not cheap.

I'd like to present a few thoughts on how to deal with these troublesome voices.

First, if you do suffer from buyer's remorse, note that you do and factor it into your decision-making process. If you know a wave of post-decision remorse is going to come your way, be prepared for it: 'Oh, it's just buyer's remorse again. I'll get over it.'

The more you study your own reactions in this case, the easier it will be to kick the remorse habit. How long does the remorse usually last? Are there any tricks you can use that are good at making it go away?

> the more you study your own reactions, the easier it will be to kick the remorse habit

Second, learn to become crystal-clear in your own mind between this essentially irrational feeling and something much more important – a sharp awareness of what is objectively wrong about your decision and how you are implementing it. The difference between the two is profound, but they can seem the same.

Remorse is essentially looking back, probably with rose-tinted spectacles, at how things were before the decision. (Going back to the Change House, it may well involve memories of the best times on the Sun Deck, and quietly skip over any denial, confusion or even despair in between those times and now.) It does not call for any action, other than a vague wish to undo the whole decision process and float back in time.

In contrast, positive awareness of weaknesses in the decision calls for specific changes to be made in how you implement it.

Buyer's remorse is somewhat like grief. When you make a major decision, it is the end of the life you had before that decision. Grief is a natural reaction to this inevitable change. Grief takes time, but after that you can lift yourself out of it by asking yourself: 'Is there an alternative way of honouring what has been lost, without feeling unhappy any more?' (See the 'positive intention' section of the troubleshooting guide on pages 120–121 for more on this question and how it works.)

brilliant example

Aileen has decided to move from a job she very much likes to a new post in a new office. She is going to honour her old job, by keeping in touch with the people she likes there on Facebook, by arranging a leaving celebration, and by e-mailing three particular colleagues and saying how much she has enjoyed working with them.

If you do find yourself stuck with an unhealthy dose of buyer's remorse, try running through the troubleshooting guide.

Get over the first hurdles neatly and elegantly

The world into which your decision pitches you – your Room of Renewal – will not be quite the world you were expecting it to be. This is because:

● your information will not have been perfect – no information is;

- the world is always changing anyway;

- your decision will itself have changed the world;

- the decision may have changed you.

Brilliant decision makers deal with this by thinking *systemically*. Any complex system is an ecology (our planet is just an extreme example of this). In such systems, changes in one part can create changes in other parts, often a long distance away (in time, in physical distance, in apparent distance down a chain of causation). A classic example is the Treaty of Versailles, which ended the First World War. Its explicit aim was to prevent Germany ever becoming nationalistic and militaristic again. In fact, it was so punitive that the German state collapsed, leading to the rise of ultra-nationalism, ultra-militarism and a new war, 20 years after the treaty was signed. Anyone who intervenes in a complex system – and any major decision is such an intervention, in the lives of yourself and other people around you – must watch out for the delayed, unpredictable, knock-on effects of their actions.

To do this, you must keep a clear track of how things are working out. This is the real job of your plans – they map out where you think you are headed; then, when reality starts taking you somewhere different, you can spot this, see what the difference is and work out what to do about it.

Some of the unexpected knock-on effects will be pleasant surprises: if you've made a good, courageous decision, good things will often come out of nowhere to support you. But there will also be unexpected difficulties. When this happens:

- Don't panic.

- Don't conclude that your decision was rubbish. It wasn't: it was imperfect, as are all decisions.

- Don't go the other way and close your eyes to the difficulty. In business, good managers 'have a nose for trouble', not so they can wallow in it (the hippo strategy) but so they can sort it out quickly and effectively.

● Realise you may have to reformulate part of your implementation plans. The aim is not to bludgeon your implementation back on to its previously agreed course, but to refine that course in the light of the new information.

● If something isn't working and you can't see why, be flexible and think 'outside the box'. Remember the complexity of the system, and that a fault in one place can show up in another. For example, a thermostat in a central heating system keeps breaking. An inept plumber replaces it with a new one, but that soon breaks. A better plumber is called, who looks at the system as a whole and spots that a bent pipe near the boiler is making the thermostat turn on and off too often so that it breaks down. Fix the cause, not the symptom.

brilliant tip

It is easier to change yourself than others. Once you have made a decision, significant others around you often notice a change in your attitude or energy. It is as if they sense you 'mean business' this time. What generally happens is that they change themselves in response to the change in you, which may then affect the way you implement your decision.

Baby steps

The art of gentle implementation also often involves the technique I call 'baby steps'. This is because many decisions are best implemented slowly.

 **example**

Helen has decided to get fit. In the past she has rushed at it, suddenly joining a gym, working out every evening – and finding her social life drying up, so that after a month or so she abandons the whole thing. Now she is planning to build the decision over time. She'll cut certain foods out of her diet straight away. She'll walk to work once a week. (A friend advised her to write down in her diary which day she is going to do this. 'Make a date with yourself and show up,' she said.) Later on, she will do the walk twice a week, join the gym and visit it twice a week.

If you make a decision to get fit the aim is that, after a while, taking time to look after your health becomes a *habit* and can gradually increase to a sensible and sustainable level. Underlying this is a change of motivation: the deep secret is to enjoy the process of looking after yourself as well as the benefits it brings. When you look forward to going for that jog, you know your fitness programme is really working.

The new behaviours that result from your decision need to become habits. Here is an exercise to bring this about.

Creating new habits

● Choose a new habit you would like to have. For example, regular exercise.

● Put in your diary. For example, two 15-minute walks one week, and a further time to plan more exercise for the following week.

● Stick to the plan for 21 days.

Stick with it

Character is the ability to carry out a worthy decision after the emotion of making that decision has passed.

Hyrum Smith, American writer and time management guru

It is often easy to begin the implementation of a decision. There's a buzz from having made a good decision and to be working on it. Things often start well, and – even if they don't – unexpected negatives get tackled with vigour and thus get sorted quickly.

Danger can come later, when things settle into more of a groove. You can 'take your eye off the ball'.

The key to long-term implementation is vision. Successful entrepreneurs and great leaders are usually very good at this. They have a vision for their business or organisation – what sort of people it serves, how it serves them, why it does this in a special way, what legacy they want to leave – and they hold fast to this.

Great leaders also inspire their vision in others. They create a shared vision, a vision they may create but which does not belong exclusively to them: other people can connect to and be inspired by it. Business writer Peter M. Senge talks about the 'sense of responsibility without possessiveness felt by leaders as stewards of their vision'.

Sometimes, you have to know when to call it a day

Sometimes a decision, however well reached, can turn out to be pushing you in the wrong direction. Reality is more complex and faster moving than any of us can model. So you need to have an awareness of when to admit that a decision has not worked and what to do if this happens.

In the Change House model, I talked about the Wrong Door. In a way, this door leads into another house – we rush out of the door, energised by our decision to do x, and are effectively in a Room of Contentment again. However, after a while things start going wrong. And, yes, we deny them. Often it takes a crisis to make us face the fact that our earlier decision hasn't worked. This is not surprising – a lot can be invested in a decision, and to turn round and accept that it has misfired can mean accepting that a lot of time and energy has been largely wasted. In practice, these won't have been wasted, as there will be many lessons we can learn – but we aren't on the nice, clear road we thought we were, and instead it's back to the Room of Confusion . . .

> often it takes a crisis to make us face the fact that our earlier decision hasn't worked

Jonathan is an entrepreneur who built up a specialist recruitment agency in the healthcare industry to over 100 staff. He felt it was time to let a more experienced manager take over, and appointed a CEO, who came highly recommended by one of Jonathan's investors. This CEO then put in a team of managers.

Happy that the agency was in safe hands, Jonathan went off and started a new business in sports hospitality – it wasn't a big earner, but he loved the new business because it enabled him to attend lots of premier sports events and meet top sportspeople (as a lad, Jonathan had played tennis to junior county level, and always secretly wanted to be a professional sportsman).

He was told that he shouldn't 'get a dog then bark himself', so he kept out of the way of the new team at the agency as much as possible, only attending monthly board meetings, where he was told everything was going fine. He noticed that a few old employees were leaving, but he was told that they were 'small business people', the kind of individuals who fitted into the slightly wild world of a growing business but not into the more efficient, process-driven machine that the new team was creating. That sounded reasonable.

Then he happened to bump into one of the ex-employees, in a check-out queue at his local supermarket. She told him that the new team was not doing a good job. The old 'all in it together' atmosphere had gone. Jonathan sympathised, but in his own mind put that down to the culture change necessary to take a business to the next stage.

At the next board meeting, he was told that the agency was having a clear-out of unprofitable customers. Some reasonably big ones were on the list: Jonathan was surprised and saddened (there were some good friends in there) – but he knew that one had to be unsentimental. He'd probably not been ruthless enough with these people, since he liked them.

Finally, one of his biggest former customers rang him up out of the blue. She complained that the new management were inflexible and unpleasant to deal with, and that if things didn't change, she would be taking her business somewhere else. She wasn't the only one, either. Did Jonathan realise what was happening? Or did he not care any longer?

Only then did Jonathan systematically ring round his old customer contacts and find out the truth about the new management – they had no feel for the business at all, and were oversimplifying what is essentially a subtle, 'people business'. Many main customers were planning on ditching them.

Time to reverse his decision. The shiny new management team had to go.

Implementation is a subtle art: this was not done instantly, with Jonathan walking in next Monday and telling the CEO and his team that they had half an hour to clear their desks. But three months later, they were all gone, apart from the FD, who turned out to be good at his job and to like working with Jonathan. And a year on from his big decision to quit the business and let 'experts' take over, Jonathan was back where he started, running the agency (he managed to get one day off to take some of the agency's top customers to Wimbledon, but in essence, the sport dream had to be put on hold: the agency had to be saved).

'You have to know when the milk has gone sour.'

Jonathan, entrepreneur

It's important to understand that Jonathan is a good decision maker who made a decision that didn't work out, not a bad decision maker. There were many good reasons for his bringing in the management team. All conventional wisdom says that this is what entrepreneurs (who are good business starters but often not good business builders) should do. The CEO came with a recommendation.

Arguably Jonathan failed to implement the decision as well as he should – he should have monitored progress more closely – but, here again, there is plenty of conventional wisdom around to the effect that once you have appointed a team, you must get off their backs and let them get on with it.

Should he have picked up warning signals earlier? Possibly, but there are usually signals of varying kinds flying around. People who have been forced out of an organisation are unlikely to be very positive about it.

Jonathan was a good decision maker because, when he saw what was really going on, he made a new decision in the light of the new information, and implemented it with appropriate speed. I'm pleased to say that the recruitment business only lost one major customer, and is making money, despite current economic conditions.

It's also important to understand that even though the original decision had to be reversed, reversing it did not take Jonathan back to where he was the day he made it. He had learnt a lot through the experience of making, then having to unwind, this decision. (I coached him, and witnessed him moving through a period of beating himself up about it, to a new place where he looks back on it all as useful learning that will make him a better entrepreneur.) The business has also progressed. The CEO did initiate some useful processes that the business could continue to use to its benefit. And a number of other people in it have become more confident and self-sufficient and generally better at their jobs, because the CEO had left them to get on with things (Jonathan had had a tendency to micro-manage). Decisions, even ones that have to be reversed, move you forward.

brilliant tip

Decisions are not like cars; even decisions that you have to reverse move you forward.

However, sometimes a decision has served its purpose and it's not so much a case of reversing it, but simply letting it come to an end.

brilliant example

James, a self-made businessman, was concerned that his 18-year-old son Daniel was growing up to be spoilt and precious. To 'toughen the kid up', he rented him a house in one of the poorest inner city areas when Daniel left home to go to university. He told Daniel to rent out the rooms and use the money to live on. This seemed to work for a while, but some of the tenants proved to be worrying. Finally, a violent tenant refused to pay the rent and threatened to beat Daniel up. Daniel became very scared. James decided to move Daniel into a small studio flat in a better part of town. James said, 'The kid has learnt his lesson. It's time to give him a break.'

🠕 brilliant recap

As you put the decision into practice, don't 'hold your decision too tight or too loose'. Get the right balance between determination to make it happen and flexibility to deal with changes that may occur:

1 Plan your implementation:
   - Put together a detailed plan of all the things you need to do.

2 Deal with the people issues:
   - Influence people who will help you implement your decision.
   - Insist on the decision if people still refuse to accept it.

3 Deal with buyer's remorse:
   - Know the difference between healthy grief that comes out of making a good decision and the negative sense of making a poor decision.

4 Get over the first hurdles neatly and elegantly:
   - Ecology – notice how the act of putting your decision into practice creates changes in unexpected ways. Learn the art of systems thinking.
   - Baby steps – build slowly towards the outcomes.

5 Stick with it:
   - Vision – after the initial euphoria, keep the dream alive.

6 Sometimes, you have to know when to call it a day:
   - If, after an appropriate period, the decision isn't working out – change it or call it a day.

CHAPTER 7

Troubleshooting guide

f, at any time in the four-stage process above, you suddenly find yourself stuck, consult this chapter to find out why – and get yourself back on track.

In essence, trouble comes from two main sources. Out there, someone or some people have an agenda for you which your decision does not fit into. Or inside you, a part of you is resisting the decision.

I shall look at both of these, starting with those agendas out there.

The world out there

We live in a world full of agendas. Everyone of any significance in our life has them for us, and the closer the person, the more powerful the agenda. This is not a recipe for paranoia. Agendas are usually fine, as they 'mesh'. Both partners in a marriage want it to work, and expect the other partner to do their bit to ensure this outcome. All the members of a sports team want to win, and they rely on each other to do their best. However, it can get more complex, especially when you decide to change. You will almost undoubtedly encounter resistance from other people in your 'agenda network' who have come to rely on you to act and react in certain ways and don't want that to change.

Remember, too, that agendas can often be hidden. Hidden agendas can be deliberately set up with dishonest intent, but they also just arise through unspoken expectations, poor communication or psychological naivety – not all hidden-agenda-holders understand what they are trying to rope other people into.

 brilliant definition

Agenda-holder

Anyone who has a role for you consciously or unconsciously scripted in their life-plan.

In all cases, there are two main ways to deal with agenda-holders:

- Getting them to change. Use the material above about influencing and insisting.
- Changing your attitude towards whatever or whoever is blocking you. I believe in balancing my needs and the needs of those who are close to me. I do not believe it is morally right to sacrifice my life for someone else, nor expect anyone else to sacrifice their life for me.

'I swear – by my life and my love of it – that I will never live for the sake of another man, nor ask another man to live for mine.'

Ayn Rand, *Atlas Shrugged*

Close family

The vast majority of people are raised not by perfect parents but by adequate parents. Sure, they got angry and occasionally went a little too far . . . But for some people, issues about family can be intractable, which is why they decide to break away. You can probably guess my view on this. Nothing your parents or wider family have given you gives them the right to control your life, which is something you must build for yourself, through your decisions: there is no more important task for any human being.

Often, absence makes the heart grow fonder, and a break of a few short months can have an amazingly positive effect on the behaviour of intransigent family members.

Both the influencing/insisting material and the change-your-attitude material in this book can be of great help when decisions get stuck due to family issues – but if the difficulties run deeper, a coach or a therapist can often have an amazingly liberating effect. It's their job to listen and help.

Close friends

This can often be a relatively agenda-free area: these people have chosen you because of who you are and want you to 'be you'. But friends can also want to rope you into an informal 'club', with rules and expected behaviours. For example, single people can get together and form a 'Single and happy' club, who meet from time to time and share horror stories about attempts at dating, and 'Aren't men/women awful?' sessions over a bottle or three of wine. Such a club has an unwritten rule: 'Don't find a long-term partner'. Another popular informal club is the 'We're overweight and we don't care' club, where the unwritten rule is 'Don't get healthy'. Even more destructive clubs are formed in bars and prisons.

If these rules are stopping you making or implementing an important decision, then maybe it's time to cancel your club membership. Remember that there will be a new club you can join – the 'Happily married' club or the 'Getting fit and enjoying it' club.

For many people, their social network can be more important than their family, so this can be quite a wrench. We all like to belong. But there's no point in belonging just for the sake of it. I believe that my friends should express their opinions, but ultimately they are there to support my decisions – that's what true friendship is all about.

If you have friends who require you to behave in destructive ways, consider the quote below:

'All you need is the right friends and the right bar – they will christen your dumpster for you!'
[A dumpster is an American word for a large dustbin on wheels.]

Bill Hicks, American comedian

At work

Ray works at a firm of City solicitors with a 'long-hours' culture. He has decided he is going to spend more time with his family, but is finding it difficult to implement this decision. He may have to make another decision: to move to a different firm and accept work that is less exciting and less well-paid.

This is not unusual: I find that employers have a habit of saying 'No' to decisions that affect them. However, if they value your contribution and they believe that their 'No' means you will leave, they may reconsider. Your influencing and political skills will come to the fore, here. If they do say 'No', it's better to give a hint of an ultimatum than to hand in your resignation at once. Use a phrase like, 'This is really very important to me and I will be very disappointed if I am prevented from doing so. Is there any way I could make it up in another way?'

Things get even worse when companies move to what appears to be indoctrination. Loyalty to an employer and a shared vision are commendable things, but when a company begins to behave like a cult – beware! I remember working at a large American multinational, and going out to lunch with a friend of my mother's. I was waxing lyrical about all the things that this company did. After a while, she said rather aggressively, 'I don't give a f*** about your employer'. I was shocked – but the more

I thought about it, the more reasonable her interjection became. I was being brainwashed: I decided to leave and set up on my own. It's worth noting that capitalism is based on the idea that the employee earns more than their salary for the employer!

Having said this, it's important to understand the full range of agendas that we bring to the workplace. People often regard work as a chore that they have to perform in order to pay the bills, but a deeper look shows that many of the things that are needed for their happiness and fulfilment are found at work.

Hidden benefits of work include:

- something to do with our time;
- the company of other people working for a common goal;
- a sense of purpose and self-respect;
- a feeling of belonging and security;
- the opportunity to learn new things and develop;
- a way of making an impact on the world, even if in a small way – making a contribution.

Some people die very shortly after retirement, because they got these benefits from work without being aware of them and failed to find alternative ways of securing the benefits after they left.

▶ brilliant example

Amy is thinking of leaving her job and setting up her own business. She feels incongruent about this. She ran through the list above, and realised that she was concerned about several of the items listed on it, especially losing the company of others and a sense of security. She decided to put more effort into organising her social life outside work, and to stay with her employer an extra six months in order to save some more money.

Other social institutions

'Passive acceptance of the teacher's wisdom is easy to most boys and girls. It involves no effort of independent thought, and seems rational because the teacher knows more than his pupils; it is moreover the way to win the favour of the teacher unless he is a very exceptional man. Yet the habit of passive acceptance is a disastrous one in later life. It causes people to seek and to accept a leader, and to accept as a leader whoever is established in that position.'

Bertrand Russell, British philosopher

The first big social institution you joined was probably your school, where you encountered plenty of agendas. Some came from teachers – the best ones wanted you to learn and grow; the mediocre ones just wanted you to shut up. The playground also offered set roles that were easy to sink into (class clown, bully, victim, show-off, etc.).

You may also have grown up in – or you may have later joined – a religious institution. I don't want to get into a long and involved discussion of these very personal issues. But the point I need to make here is that our perceptions of our roles, our beliefs and our values can be changed – not like clothes, to suit a mood, but to suit deep changes in our awareness of who we are and what we have to do with our lives. There will be more on this later in this chapter.

> our perceptions of our roles, our beliefs and our values can be changed

Experts

Society is full of these, and they all have powerful agendas: 'Respect my expertise'; 'Do as I say, not what I do – and don't ask questions'. Many claim greater knowledge than they actually have.

This can be particularly important when a decision takes you into a new area of knowledge (or lack of it, to start with). You need to develop clear criteria by which to judge who is a real expert and who just goes round claiming to be one. Letters after the name are not sufficient criteria. Talk to other people on a similar journey to yourself. Read widely. Above all, retain a critical mindset.

Watch out for 'expert overstretch'. People who are genuinely expert in one part of a field become overconfident and start lecturing the world about other aspects of that field (or other areas of expertise altogether). Because they have a track record of excellence in their original area, people don't dare to criticise them.

Watch out also for the hallmarks of the overrated expert: the strident tone, the refusal to listen to argument, the insistence that you either totally agree with them or you're an idiot, the cult of the personality ('My ego, right or wrong').

The media

'One of the most valuable philosophical features of journalism is that it realises that truth is not solid but a fluid.'

Christopher Morley, British journalist

The people and organisations who bombard us through the various media have enormous agendas that have precious little to do with our private, personal well-being. Newspapers are in business to sell newspapers, not to improve the world – and certainly not to help you make brilliant decisions. TV companies have to sell advertising (or justify their licence fee). Even great artists are interested in expressing themselves rather than helping *you*.

These institutions, commercial and cultural, can shape us at every level – which is fine if we choose it, but not if they just smuggle beliefs and values into our heads that stop us making the decisions that are good for us.

Possessions

'Be the master of your possessions; don't let your possessions be the master of you.'

My father, Irwin Steinhouse

In our society we acquire a lot of stuff: a house, a car, furniture, pictures, clothes, fancy electrical goods . . . and so on. These can end up blocking our decisions as effectively as difficult individuals; people get trapped by possessions.

Part of the solution is sensible management. Can you rent your home? Can you store your car somewhere safe? Can you put your treasured possessions in an affordable, safe storage facility?

Possessions often signify much more than they appear to. Clearly, some goods have sentimental value. Another way they acquire value is as a symbol of freedom. When we are young, our parents usually control our access to money. At a certain age we express our independence by being able to spend our money how we want. Ask yourself if it has now come to a time when that great independent feeling of buying and having stuff is actually a weight around your neck.

Inside: the psychology of getting unstuck

Some decisions get stuck because of inconsistencies in ourselves. This might seem painful and inconvenient – but it can also be seen as an opportunity for change. If you really want to do something but a part of you is objecting, you have an excellent opportunity to look at this part and find out why. What message is the objecting part sending you? Why is it doing that? Do you still wish to be the sort of person that part wants you to be?

I shall look at various ways in which we can feel bad about decisions, and provide some ideas and exercises to overcome these.

My decision clashes with my vocation

If you have an obvious mission in life, it's unlikely you will make decisions that run counter to it. But many people have a vocation (a 'mission' or a 'calling', if you prefer) but don't really realise the fact. Getting stuck on a big decision can often make them aware of this vocation for the first time.

This may sound a bit odd, but as a coach I have seen this happen many times. People suddenly become aware of 'what they want to do with their lives'. At the same time they also realise they have at some level known this for a while, but haven't wanted to face up to it (in the Change House model, they have been sitting in the Room of Denial).

A common area where people get stuck in this way is a decision about a change of workplace or a promotion. The decision looks a 'no-brainer' on the outside, but something doesn't feel right.

 **example**

Sandra worked as an accountant for a freight company. She was offered promotion and felt she deserved it, but still felt uneasy about accepting it. Why? Her real passion in life was for exercise and she spent most of her spare time in the gym and working as a personal trainer at weekends. But the personal training work did not pay well, and she had developed a strategy of doing the day job to pay for the activities that she loved. She talked the matter of the promotion over with a friend one weekend, and realised that in accepting it she felt she was committing herself more to the day job, and that in her heart that was not what her life was about. What she loved was the personal training – helping other people get fit. She decided to change jobs and apply for an accountancy post at a health club. This did mean a cut in pay, but she could live on this. The new job made her feel that her work as well as her leisure was devoted to her calling of helping people – including herself – become healthier.

As I've said, having a mission and not knowing it sounds odd – but I have met a lot of people in that situation. It is worth trying to create some kind of 'mission statement' for yourself – though please avoid the ghastly 'managementese' that businesses use when they try to do this. Have a mission statement like Sandra's: 'To help people get healthier'.

I talk about this in another book, *Think Like an Entrepreneur*. I also have recorded a free MP3 on www.thinklikean entrepreneur.com, which will talk you through how to craft such a statement.

Yes, but is it really me?

People often decide to do something, but then run up against a very strong feeling that, though it's a good idea in theory and would suit other people, to do it would not be 'them'. 'I don't do x: I'm just not that sort of person.' This is, of course, healthy if x is the decision is to do something foolish. But supposing x is to do something worthwhile, that your head and your heart want?

Here, the decision is clashing with your deep feelings of identity. These feelings are visceral – the 'gut feel' question at the end of the decision simulator is essentially about identity. They are often irrational and yet hugely powerful. They can be amazingly supportive in tough times, but also pernicious: throughout history millions of people have died in conflicts about identity.

A particularly painful way in which feelings of identity can block decision making is via a 'double bind', one of these Catch 22 (damned if you do and damned if you don't) situations.

brilliant example

Keith comes from a rich family, but does not get on with his parents. 'I don't want to be a rich b****** like my dad,' he says. But, at the same time, he likes to see himself as sharp and streetwise. 'I'm a bit of an entrepreneur,' he says later, and tells me about a deal he did recently where he cleared five grand for a week's work. He then often blows the money on pointless bets or drugs because, having made the money, he suddenly hates it. In order to come to a congruent decision about his life and where it is headed, he must sort out 'who he is'.

So what can we do about this?

As notions of identity are often set in our unconscious minds early and stay there, exercising an influence of which we are not aware, simply bringing them to our conscious awareness can allow us to question them and decide to change them. Identity, though powerful, is not as fixed as some people think.

brilliant example

Martin looks back with affection at the time when he decided to stop seeing himself as a hell-raiser and to become a parent, long-term partner and a success at his work. This was a conscious decision he made, on a particular day, and he actually said to himself: 'I am not that kind of person any longer.' He did so in a spirit of gratitude to the past. The hell-raising had been fun, but it was time to move on.

It can help to write down a list of our identities, and to return to this over time and edit it.

We can choose not to take on identities. When Renée Zellweger was cast as Bridget Jones, she went on an anti-diet, fattening up for the role. Did she become 'a fat person' in that time? Not unless she chose to think of herself as that.

A really pernicious double-bind is best sorted out with the help of a coach or therapist.

'Our deepest fear is not that we are inadequate. Our deepest fear is that we are powerful beyond measure. It is our light, not our darkness, that most frightens us. We ask ourselves, who am I to be brilliant, gorgeous, talented and fabulous? Actually, who are you not to be . . .? We are all meant to shine, as children do. And as we let our own light shine, we unconsciously give other people permission to do the same. As we are liberated from our own fear, our presence automatically liberates others.'

Marianne Williamson, American writer and spiritual activist

I don't know why – but I just feel I'm not allowed to make this decision

This may sound odd: we're adults; we can do what we choose (as long as we accept the consequences). But many of us have old beliefs about what we may or may not do lurking in our unconscious mind from childhood. A decision to do new things can clash with this ancient stuff – and if we do not challenge it, the ancient stuff can win!

Here's a brief exercise to break the spell of lacking permission.

Granting permission

1   Write down what you want permission to do as a simple statement of intent. For example, 'I'm going to start my own business'.

2   Write down all the *negative* consequences if you do not put your statement of intent into action. For example: 'I'll spend the rest of my life feeling I never reached my true potential.' 'I'll

remain stuck in the IT department, when there are so many other aspects of business I want to learn about.' 'I'll become envious of people who make it.'

3   Write down all the *positive* consequences if you do not put your statement of intent into action. For example: 'As an employee, I get a regular wage.' 'Some of my current work is quite interesting.' 'It's secure.'

4   Work out how many of the things in step 3 above are 'must haves' and how many are just 'would likes'.

5   For the 'must haves', work out how you could get these benefits, and *also* achieve what you want.

6   Now, say to yourself in front of a mirror: 'I give myself permission to do x', where x is your statement of intent in step 1 above. Say this in a special way. 'I give myself permission to *start my own business*.' Emphasise the words in italic; as you say them, make eye contact with yourself and speak louder and clearer. This may feel a little odd, but you are actually doing a bit of NLP on yourself, sending yourself what is called an 'embedded command'.

7   How does that feel? If you do not feel a change, go back to step 4 and consider what else you need to do to satisfy your objections. Then repeat steps 5 and 6 and give yourself permission again. Repeat this process until you feel a *real energy surge*. Permission granted!

I just don't think I can carry this decision out.

If you believe it is impossible for you to achieve a set of outcomes, my first question to you is: 'What stops you?' The answer is usually some kind of belief.

People often hold beliefs to protect themselves. A classic example is, 'I shall never fall in love again, because

people often hold beliefs to protect themselves

I got hurt so much the last time'. (Note the giveaway word 'never': this belief is dangerously rigid.) For a while, that belief may well offer protection, but the cost can be excessive. The time will come to question the belief. Ask yourself: 'Is this belief still useful?' or 'Does it still serve me?'

When you do this, it is essential to honour the original purpose of the belief by finding other protective mechanisms, such as getting to know a person much better before you decide to have a relationship with them, or being much more choosy and selective (and so on).

The starting point of questioning a belief can be to recognise that's what it is: a belief you hold, not an objective and unalterable fact about the universe. Instead of just asserting the belief, say, 'A belief that I choose to hold is ...'.

Widen your horizons. Get new perspectives on the belief you hold. Other people seem to flourish without believing it ... Talk the issue through with friends, or a coach. Read; for example, the hurt lover above would do well to pick up a volume of Victorian poetry and read 'Tis better to have loved and lost / Than never to have loved at all' (Tennyson, *In Memoriam*).

Beliefs checklist

Do any of the following assertions about life fit your beliefs?

1   Life is tough. It's a dog-eat-dog world and you've got to fight for your piece of it. I don't really trust anyone else.

2   Life is uncertain. I am scared that things will go wrong and I won't be able to cope.

3   Life is unfair. There are so many wars, so much poverty and problems with the environment, that it would be morally wrong to feel happy with all of this going on.

4   Life is mystical. There is a force that really controls everything in life; I have no significant power over my destiny.

5   Life is a struggle. I don't have enough money; people who do are crooks and I will not join them.

6   Life is theirs. My parents, partner, boss, social group, children, society and religion dictate how I must lead my life. I would be a bad person if I did things for myself. I have no real choice.

7   Life is thinking. My mind gives me the choice to control and feel anything I want; if I feel bad it is simply because I have had a lapse in thinking.

8   Life is a joke. If I don't take it seriously and don't engage, I can have a laugh and not get hurt.

9   Life is a party. I will enjoy myself as much as possible and live every day like my last, as one day it will be. If my body gives out, at least I won't get old.

10   Life is a tragedy. It always ends in tears.

Do you have a belief like one of the above that is currently blocking your decisions? Do you wish to change that belief? Create your own, more positive and realistic metaphor for life. I like:

Life is a story. I have influence over what goes on; however I can enjoy witnessing the journey unfold whatever happens and receive valuable learning along the way.

Produce your own.

Changing beliefs

Beliefs can be changed. Ask yourself these questions:

1   What is the belief that is blocking your decision? *(Jim is trying to lose weight. But he has a belief that 'thin people are boring'.)*

2   What would you like to believe? *(Jim comes up with: 'You can be thin and have fun.')*

3   Think of something you used to believe. *(Jim recalls 'Life is about getting as many sweets as possible.')*

4   How do you feel about that old belief, now? *(That's silly!)*

5   So – you've seen that beliefs can change! *(Yes!)*

6   Now, is there anything stopping you changing the blocking belief? *(My friends in the 'We're overweight and we don't care' club won't like me any more.)*

7   Is there anything you can do about whatever is stopping you? *(If some of my friends don't accept it, I will find some new ones.)*

8   Listen extra carefully to this one. What is more important to you: gaining the new belief and the benefits it will bring, or not dealing with the problems caused by changing the blocking belief? *(Gaining the new belief. I really want to move on.)*

9   Think again about the old blocking belief. Can you now look at it with the same affection as you do when you think of x? [Insert whatever you said in answer to step 3 above.] *(Yes, I think I can . . .)*

Is your decision a dilemma?

Many decisions can get blocked because values are clashing, and we can't work out which value matters most. Common dilemmas are between honest self-interest and the interests of others: both these values are 'good' – but when they clash, which one should I follow?

It is always wise to have a hierarchy of values in your own mind.

Prioritising your values

1 Write down a list of your values.

2 Elaborate a little on each one – what does this value mean to you? Be as personal as you like. For example, on my own list one of my key values is 'Wisdom', which I then elaborate by saying 'Distil learning into a life-changing experience'. The original model for this process is the 'Thirteen Virtues' of American statesman Benjamin Franklin.

3 Put them in an order of priority. This may feel a little artificial, but do it anyway. And do it a number of times. As with so many things, once you have asked your unconscious mind to work on this issue, it will do so. Check in from time to time to see where it has got to.

Doing this exercise regularly may well end up with you having a very different set of values. A friend did this and suddenly realised that many of the values he had originally written down were his father's, and that he did not really believe in them.

Your hierarchy will not solve every dilemma – the choice between a minor infringement of a major value and a major infringement of a lesser value will not be automatic – but it helps in many value clashes.

Once you have decided, consider what you can do to pursue the goal you have selected while honouring, as far as possible, the value you have rejected.

brilliant example

Jane has been given the opportunity to do some very interesting work in Paris. Her mother wants her to stay in Luton. Jane is an only child ... but does that really mean she must stay in Luton? She decides to go to Paris, but makes commitments to her mother that she will return to Luton every month, phone every week and come over specially for her birthday.

The Golden Rule ('treat people as you would have them treat you') can help in this kind of decision: 'If the roles were reversed, would I expect the other person to make this sacrifice for me?'

Sometimes, of course, there can be no honouring. Breaking off a significant relationship can be like this.

A story related by motivational speaker Hyrum Smith involves a man whose boss – a person whom the man greatly admired – offered him promotion to the board, as long as he would always support his boss's decisions regardless of whether he agreed with them or not. There was no middle way here. The man had to decide between loyalty and integrity. For him, integrity was a more important value than loyalty, so he turned down the offer and left the company. He started his own business (which grew to be a world-beater).

I feel very strongly that everybody needs to have their own moral code that is personal and unique to them. The world is full of exhortations that seem to pull in different directions – 'Don't look a gift horse in the mouth' versus 'All that glitters is not gold' – and you have to plot your course between them. You can learn from other people and institutions, but the final deep truth is to create a code of your own. If you follow someone else's code, you will not be able to make truly congruent decisions.

Do you lack the skills to implement the decision?

'Anything worth doing well is worth doing badly to start with.'

Attributed to many people, including British novelist
G.K. Chesterton

Arguably, the more radical and life-changing the decision, the more likely it is to pitch you into implementation issues where you have very little skill. Great! Accept this, and relish the challenge of acquiring these skills.

Remember that all learning is challenging and can take time to master. Accept the fact that you will suddenly be surrounded by people who have been doing whatever it is for years and who make it look easy. Remember that they were learners once, too.

Learning tends to advance according to a set pattern. Many people begin with *unconscious incompetence* – they think it's easy. Then they try, and realise it's hard: *conscious incompetence*. Through practice, they become better, though they have to keep concentrating to ensure good performance (*conscious competence*). Finally, they have mastered whatever it is, and do it without thinking – *unconscious competence*.

Wealth and health can only be achieved via learning and practising new skills and attitudes. To gain and maintain them require time and effort. As an entrepreneur, it took me a long time to acquire all the

> wealth and health can only be achieved via learning and practising new skills and attitudes

skills needed to build and maintain wealth. Likewise Tony Felix, my fitness coach, took many years building his body, fitness and the disciplines needed to maintain them. He once said to me, 'You must have taken a lot of effort getting a nice home to live in; why not put some effort into building a nice body to live in, too?' That was ten years ago, and I am still learning all the things I need to master to achieve excellent health.

Have I got the energy to carry out my decision?

A major change in your life can be draining physically: are you keeping fit amid all these changes? Or are you snacking and not getting enough exercise?

Positive intention

I have alluded to this in the section on beliefs above, and would like to expand on it a little here. The concept of *positive intention* states that any of the thought or behaviour patterns in our mind were originally put there by us for a good reason. If the thought or behaviour seems bizarre and unhelpful now, that is because the context has changed radically. Around five years old, we are still very small, but eager to make sense of the world. We see the world 'magically', and often in terms of clashing extremes. We don't understand the finality of death. But we are also vulnerable, in great need of love and often afraid. We need to find ways to ensure parental love and at the same time to put up barriers that will protect ourselves. These 'routes to love' and these barriers can often take very odd forms, for example:.

● My parents will only love me if I'm stupid.

● I'll only be safe if I never say what I really feel to anyone.

As adults, our understanding deepens, but the original love-ensuring and protective mechanisms often stay in place, now hopelessly out of date and unhelpful, but still perceived by the psyche as necessary. In seeking to remove such outdated mind-patterns, we have to understand the jobs they were originally created to do, and find a way of doing those jobs in a more relevant, effective, adult way.

How do you find love now? How do you protect yourself now?

As I hope I have shown in this chapter, decisions can often be blocked by irrational thought patterns, and the best way to remove such blocks is to find out what their original positive intention was and to replace them with something that still fulfils that purpose but in a realistic, contemporary way. Simply exposing their oddness to rational thought won't make them go away: the psyche still says, 'Yes, they're crazy, but I need them'.

brilliant example

A coaching client, Joan, a lady in her mid fifties, told me she hated smoking but couldn't quit. I asked her what good things (positive intentions) she got out of smoking. 'None,' she replied. 'I hate it, but I'm hooked.'

Nicotine is similar to caffeine – the addiction is physically quite easy to overcome: it's the psychology that hooks people. I pressed Joan for the positive intentions of her smoking, and after a while she gave a long list, including a break, a treat, a way to unwind and a social life with other smokers standing outside her workplace. She also said she started smoking at 15: she was a rebel and it made her feel like a grown-up woman. With all these reasons, is it any wonder she found it hard to give up?

Finding alternative ways to satisfy these positive intentions allows the unconscious mind to let go of these needs. Joan said she no longer needed to smoke to maintain her identity as a bit of a rebel now that she was a woman at 55 (interestingly, she said that she needed to tell someone that fact before she could let it go). With the other issues, she came up with alternative strategies for her to relax, have treats, etc. After the session she finally managed to give up and has not been smoking since.

Simple mislabelling of feelings

People often shy away from big decisions because they are afraid of the consequences. Maybe you are facing a big decision and feeling that way right now. If so, are you sure that what you are feeling is fear? The physiological symptoms of fear and excitement are very similar.

Often we are taught to label a set of physiological events as fear when it is actually excitement. We then compound this mistake by associating lots of 'fear' memories with the feeling when it comes up again.

To misquote self-help author Susan Jeffers: 'Feel the excitement and do it anyway!'

↗ brilliant recap

The troubleshooting guide helps when you get 'stuck':

1 The problem can appear to come from the world out there:
- Objections from family and friends.
- Not fitting into the agenda at work or in other institutions.
- Getting conflicting advice from experts or the media.
- Worries about losing our possessions.

2 We can often find the solution by changing our attitudes or approach to:
- Our vocation – balancing what we want to do with our life and making a living.
- Who we are – updating who we think we are and what we are allowed to do.
- What is possible – changing the way we see the world and our place in it.
- Conflicting issues – finding out what is truly important so we can deal with dilemmas.
- Lack of skills – learning new capabilities and behaviours.
- Lack of energy – keeping fit to get the job done.

3 Two other tools can help to unstick a decision:
- The principle of positive intention – replacing out-of-date ways of securing benefits with better ways.
- The phenomenon of the mislabelling of feelings – fear and excitement are very similar!

PART 3

Contexts

n this part of the book I answer a number of common questions about decision making. How do I practise? Why are some people brilliant at decision making in some areas and poor in others (and what can they do about this)? What about decision making in groups?

Finally, I look at an analogy between decision making and a model of personal change that is used with equal power in deep therapy work and when people write scripts for Hollywood.

CHAPTER 8

Practice makes brilliant

'An expert is someone who has made every mistake possible in a very narrow field.'
          Niels Bohr, Danish physicist and Nobel Prize winner

The most important factor in becoming a good decision maker is practice. Malcolm Gladwell's book, *Outliers*, argues that to master anything, you need to spend 10,000 hours on it. Can you do this for your decision making?

Probably not. But can you get in as much practice as you can? Yes!

There is a problem, however: pure decision-making practice is hard to come by. Learning the drums, I spent many hours bashing a practice kit in my garage, where nobody but me could hear. If I made mistakes, I might get a bit upset, but nobody else was troubled. Then I joined a band and rehearsed in another garage. If I made mistakes, it now inconvenienced four other people – luckily I had enough resilience to take any criticism and get playing again (they all made mistakes, too, so it evened out over a few sessions). Finally, I got out in front of an audience and actually performed. There, if I'd made a lot of mistakes, it would have spoiled the evenings of the people at the event – but by that time I'd practised enough so that didn't happen.

Decision making isn't like this. It's almost all 'real-time', out there in front of other people from the start. There is no 'garage' to practise in. We just have to get out there and make mistakes.

The inactivity trap

For most people, the need for practice is unwelcome but bearable. We just accept the fact and get on with it. Humour is a great protector at this point. However for others, fear of failure and of shame can be overwhelming. Such fears can plunge the individual into a vicious circle. You fear making mistakes, so you don't try anything. As a result, you don't learn anything. Meanwhile your peers are out there experimenting, getting it wrong, learning and growing their skill base. The gap between what they can do and what you can do grows ever wider. A first, fumbling venture into reality, which (you now realise) would have been par for the course five years ago, would now look absolutely ridiculous, so you retreat even further into your shell . . .

This cycle of inactivity and fear of action must be broken. The troubleshooting material can help here. Many people imprison themselves in this circle with beliefs, such as 'People who make mistakes are stupid'. Challenge these beliefs. Who says this? Supposing they are wrong?

Another dangerously self-limiting belief is 'I must be perfect'. Who says you must be perfect? Why must you be perfect? Isn't being perfect actually dull and lifeless? Life is a big, exciting adventure, not a tiny little exercise in perfection.

brilliant tip

Brilliant decision makers do not expect perfection from themselves or others.

The desire to be perfect can be attacked by asking: 'What does being perfect do for you?'

If the answer is another mental state, like 'It makes me feel safe', use the concept of *positive intention* and ask: 'Are there any other ways you can feel safe?'

Or the reply might be: 'It means people won't think I am stupid.' But 'people' is a generalisation, and needs to be questioned: 'Which people specifically?'

The answer may be an evasion: 'Oh, I don't know. People. Everybody.' In this case, keep pressing for specific answer. Or it might be specific. 'My parents' is a common one. In this case, ask: 'What good thing do you get if your parents think you are not stupid?'

A common answer is: 'It makes me feel I am lovable.' You can either use the positive intention question again – 'Are there any other ways you can feel you're lovable?' – or challenge the belief behind the answer: 'Do you think if someone else makes a mistake they are unlovable?'

Usually after a bout of this kind of interrogation, the belief that we have to be perfect begins to crumble. It won't go away in one session of questioning, but regular assaults on it will release you from its irrational power.

The right way, of course, to use mistakes is to learn from them – as we saw Garry Kasparov do.

> the right way to use mistakes is to learn from them

Another enemy of getting out there and making a few mistakes is *loss aversion*. The mind may well dwell excessively on any losses incurred in this process – or even potential losses. Don't let it. Here, the wild Platonic horses of your unconscious mind have actually become droopy and listless. Get the charioteer cracking the whip; make your reason override any excessive dwelling on loss.

As you practise your decision making, watch – in precise detail – what you actually do. As we saw in Chapter 5 on making the decision, everybody has their own 'micro-strategy' for deciding. Choosing food in a quiet restaurant is an ideal opportunity to do this. You check the food item. Do you make a picture of it? Do you recall a memory when you last ate the item? Do you remember a feeling you had when you last ate it? Do you check all the items in the menu before you narrow it down to three or four choices? Do you consider how you might feel after eating this meal? Become curious about how you think in these comfortable situations and you will be able to use this information as an aid to more complex and pressing decisions.

brilliant tip

Study how you make small decisions in as much detail as you can. Whatever process you discover clearly works for you, consider using it when making big decisions.

Entrepreneurship

I can't think of a better way to practise decision making than running your own business. I don't necessarily mean setting out to be the next Richard Branson or Anita Roddick – though if that's what you want, go for it! Even a small part-time business will force you to make decisions on a regular basis.

brilliant tip

Your own small business is a great place to learn the art of decision making.

Most of these decisions will be quite small, which is what you want as a 'learner'. There will be plenty of them – from which stapler to buy to whether to take a piece of business from a person you know to be a slow payer. You will have to make these decisions in a clear time frame: you can't dawdle. And they will be your decisions, affecting you and your business and not much else.

Another advantage of learning decision making through enterprise is that you will find it easy to get a good mentor, who will help you learn. The concept of mentoring is well understood in the business world and there are various schemes to provide mentoring for start-ups. Check out organisations like your local Chamber of Commerce or Business Link to see what they offer.

Here's a great example of the importance of decision making in the entrepreneurial business. Note that the decisions involved were small ones, not giant 'Shall we take over IBM?' ones.

---

brilliant example

Brian, the founder of a retailing business, decided he wanted to take a sabbatical. He appointed Patrick, his finance director, to the role of managing director. Patrick was a very thorough individual, who spent a long time considering possible outcomes before making any decision. His motto was: 'I like to know everything about something before I give my opinion.' After the promotion, Patrick worked in his usual manner. Papers began piling up in his office. Staff became anxious, as they were not being given instructions; instead they were simply told to wait. After a few months, the pile of paper had grown waist high and Patrick was becoming so stressed with all the outstanding decisions that less and less was being decided upon. When Brian returned from his sabbatical, he was horrified at what had happened and immediately took over the reins again.

Remember the motto 'Perfect is the enemy of done'. If you do have this desire for perfection, you really need to flush it out and change it before you start a small business.

In the fast-moving world of business, some decisions need to be taken quickly, even if they turn out to be mistaken. This book shows how you can make decisions in such a way that you increase your chances of undoing major mistakes.

I find as an entrepreneur that most decisions can be made or agreed with other people relatively quickly: this leaves vital time to think in depth about big decisions, and to get advice or coaching to make the right big choices.

CHAPTER 9

Making brilliant decisions in all areas of life

I hope that one of the key messages you have got from this book is that decision making is one of the most important life skills anyone can have. And I do mean anyone, not just business people. How we make decisions affects how we lead our lives – in all areas, not just business but also relationships, health and lifestyle.

I believe that decision making is a 'general' skill, by which I mean that once you have mastered it in one area of your life, you can transfer it *reasonably easily* to another area. As you practise decision making, you become brilliant at how to plan a decision, how to check for congruence, how to unblock yourself, how to deal with buyer's remorse, how to implement gently and flexibly (and many other skills). These skills will serve you wherever you choose to exercise them – be it investing on the stock market, asking someone out on a date, setting up a business, buying a car or getting fit.

However, I have noticed that many people seem oddly unable to transfer their decision making skills from one area to another.

 **examples**

- Ray is a successful lawyer, with a busy practice. He keeps fit, working out regularly and playing squash in winter and cricket in the summer. His personal life ... a disaster. He has been married twice – he's good with money, and would be well off were it not for two sets of alimony payments. He is now actually dating two women at the same time and not telling either of them this is the case.

- Sally is single, too, but happy that way. She plans to be married by 30, but right now is too busy having fun. She is good at choosing friends, and at cultivating her relationships with those who prove worthy of her friendship and at ditching, in as polite a way as possible, those who do not. But ... she has problems holding down a job, and has recently put on several stone. She is also in debt.

> **failings in one area of life will undo all the good work in other areas**

You could look at the two individuals in the examples above and say, 'That's life. Nobody's perfect.' True, but both these people are clearly letting themselves down in a way that they can and should be able to sort. And if they do not address their problems, things will get worse for them and their failings in one area of life will drag them down and undo all the good work they have done in the other areas.

What should Sally and Ray do? They need to accept that they make poor decisions in these areas, and that they need to take the decision-making skills they clearly have in some areas of their life and transfer them to the problem areas.

Coaches use a technique called the coaching wheel. The wheel looks like this. It usually has eight segments, though there's no

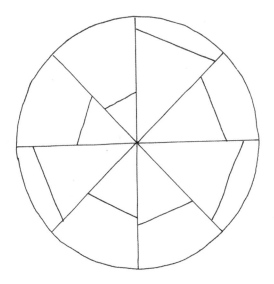

real reason why, other than because it looks neat. But life isn't always neat: if you want seven segments, or ten, have them!

You then allocate a segment to each significant area of your life. For example:

- career
- money
- health
- friends and family
- significant other/romance
- personal growth
- fun and recreation
- physical environment.

Then grade your life as it is right now (*not* how you would like it to be) for each segment. 10 is top score; 1 is a low score. Grade it according to your aspirations: for health a 10 is not an Olympic athlete, but what you would consider to be super fit for yourself. Don't think about each answer for long – do this fast;

a minute or two should complete the whole exercise. Trust your unconscious to come up with the gradings, and don't override it with what you think you 'ought' to be rated at.

Here's a sample wheel filled in.

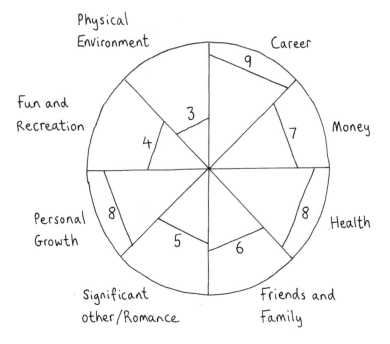

Rather than create a balanced wheel, people often work hard on creating as imbalanced a wheel as possible, concentrating all their resources on those areas at which they are already good or even excellent – the mistakes that Ray and Sally have been making.

This is a phenomenon I encounter a lot as a coach. People come to me wanting to become better at some area of their life. As we talk, it becomes apparent that they are actually pretty competent in this area – their real problems lie elsewhere. But they do not see the problem area as a problem, or – very common – as worthy of serious personal work.

When they realise this, they are often filled with fear, and it's my (very rewarding) job to help them through this.

brilliant tip

Don't spend all your energy, effort and time on getting even better at the things you are good at already. Put some of these resources into shoring up your weaknesses.

There are almost always deep, personal reasons why otherwise competent people choose not to make good decisions in particular areas of their life. These reasons are of the kind we looked at in the troubleshooting guide. In money matters, people have all sorts of barriers to success: 'Rich people are b******s.'; 'I'm not the sort of person who has loads of money.' In relationships it is often about whether we deserve love. In health, people decide they are not sporty, so ignore health altogether.

brilliant example

Natasha, an Oxford graduate, had a clear view of herself as an intellectual. The bank where she worked entered a team for the London Marathon. She did not want to participate, but perceived that joining the team would help her career. The team was also raising money for a charity assisting farmers in Rwanda, which she very much supported. Once the training began, she found her perception of 'who she was' changing – she could be both sporty and intelligent. She completed the event in 4 hours 56 minutes.

Interestingly, this led to a number of changes in Natasha's life, including a greater feeling of ease at her work, where there was quite a macho culture – something she can now handle with greater ease.

People who concentrate on one or two areas of the wheel often feel completely lost when contemplating other aspects.

▶ brilliant example

Sarah is a successful entrepreneur. She started in business in her teens and now in her early forties employs 600 people in four countries. Although she has all the material signs of success – a large house and an expensive car – she has not had a lasting relationship for many years. She is also very overweight and says she has no time to exercise and just 'grabs food on the run'. She has said that she could have chosen to get married and have children, but would then not have been able to succeed in business. Asked now what she wants, she gives a huge and very weary shrug and says: 'I don't know. I've worked so hard that all of the problems in the business have gone away; but I have no idea what I want for myself.'

Sarah is typical of the belief that 'If you have x, you can't have y'. She needs to question this: the belief that you need completely to sacrifice a family or your health to succeed in your career is simply wrong. There are plenty of examples of successful people who have had happy families and remained healthy.

At the same time, I don't believe the mantra of some coaches – that you can 'have it all'. Not filled up to 10 in the wheel, you can't. But you can set to work on those areas where your grading is low and start working on getting them to a 6 or a 7.

Remember 'baby steps'.

 **example**

Adrian is a very successful solicitor, a partner in a large international law firm. He spent little time at home with his wife, Sandra, and their children, William and Sarah. The time he did spend, he found frustrating; partly for that reason he worked even longer hours. After a harsh childhood, one of his stated beliefs was 'People need to look after themselves, no whingeing'. Sandra became very ill with a chest infection, and he didn't even visit her in hospital. When she came back and complained, he told her to 'Grow up and live with it'.

After Sandra threatened to leave him, Adrian ended up in therapy. Working on small steps, such as asking Sandra how her day was, listening without judging or offering advice, showing his feelings and expressing his needs in conversation, Adrian improved his relationship with his wife, and his children started to do better at school. He later remarked that it didn't need much extra time to change his home life, just a different way of seeing the world and behaving. Sometimes, a small change of effort and focus in an 'Achilles' heel' area can make a remarkable difference.

I said that decision-making skills are 'reasonably easy' to transfer from one part of your life to another (assuming the big psychological blocks have been moved out of the way). This does not mean they are instantly transferable, the way you soon learn to drive one brand of car after having driven a different brand for a while. It's deeper than that. You have to start slowly in your new area, making a few small, simple decisions and then building up to the big ones, learning as you do so the specific 'how tos' of deciding in this area.

But in the end, your skills will transfer across.

CHAPTER 10

Brilliant group decision making

This book has so far focused mainly on how you as an individual can make decisions. However, in life we often make decisions along with other people. This can range from you and one other person, through teams, to voting for a decision.

I must express a core belief here: decisions by committee don't work.

That does not mean that decision makers in group contexts, such as business leaders, have to be dictatorial. The keys to good group decisions lie in having a leader and in having everyone else in the group contribute to the decision in the best way.

brilliant tip

The best group decisions are made where the group has a leader – but where the leader listens very carefully to what the group members have to say.

Brilliant group decisions happen when people within a group feel secure enough to express their views, especially when they oppose a decision. Yet there still needs to be one person who is responsible for making the decision. Group decision making then becomes similar to the activities of researching and of creating and evaluating options covered in Stage 2 of the four-stage process (see Chapter 4). There is one decision maker who calls upon other individuals to learn and inform him or her about issues and potential pitfalls.

Working in groups

The group leader does not have to make every decision. In fact they shouldn't. They should delegate. If there is someone who is an expert in their field, they can often be given the responsibility for making decisions in that area. The subject should be discussed by everyone beforehand, but in the end the expert decides. As with all brilliant decisions, the decision should be as flexible as possible.

Different people in the team should play different roles, depending on their temperament and skill. There are various models for team roles. The one created by Meredith Belbin is the classic.

In his model, the group needs the following people:

- Shaper – the leader.
- Co-ordinator – keeps the personal balance of the team (the shaper can offend and override quieter members).
- Plant – not the lead singer of Led Zeppelin but a generator of ideas.
- Resource investigator – finds out new opportunities and information.
- Company worker – is familiar with the organisational context in which the decision is being made and will ensure it has a smooth transition to general acceptance.
- Monitor-evaluator – carefully evaluates options.
- Team worker – like the co-ordinator, unruffles feathers if egos have run wild.

- Completer-finisher – ensures that the decision covers all options and is implemented in detail.
- Specialist – a subject-matter expert.

This model is useful, but it assumes rather a large group. It is also something of an ideal – get nine people in a room and you are very unlikely to get this breakdown of temperaments and abilities.

A simpler model comes from the work of Robert Dilts, who analysed the leadership style of great entrepreneurs. He found that these people often played three roles:

- Dreamer – has the vision and comes up with ideas.
- Realist – puts the ideas into practice.
- Critic – a positive critic, not a spoiler, who looks for problems so they can be met head on.

A good team should have at least one person who plays each of these roles.

In business, often people in sales are the dreamer, people in finance the critic, and people in operations the realist. In a family, often the children are dreamers, the father the critic and the mother the realist. But don't be bound by this. You know your group.

Remember that roles are not identity. If you are playing one of these roles, make sure you don't start turning into it. Try playing a different role in group discussions at home to the one you play at work.

brilliant tip

The ideal group for decision making consists of at least three people, playing the roles of dreamer, realist and critic.

Part of the skill of the leader is that of influencing – making sure that the rest of the group buys into the decision. The more they have been listened to and generally involved, for example as providers of information on a particular aspect, the more likely that is to happen: the team feels involved in the decision-making process and that the decision is partly theirs.

If you are in this leadership position, ensure that you start the whole process off with the right intention – to solve the problem in a way that people can buy into, not to 'get your way'. In NLP we say that 'energy follows intention' – starting off with the right end in mind is the best way of getting there.

> starting off with the right end in mind is the best way of getting there

Such leaders can, in my view, be described as being democratic, even if they have the final say. Democracy, remember, is not a series of endless referenda: we vote for people we think will make good decisions, then let them get on with it, under regular scrutiny via the media.

Decisions for two

Allocating decisions between equal partners is often best done by finding out how important the decision is to each of you. If I sense that my wife, business partner or children consider something to be vitally important while I don't, then I usually pass on the decision to them. Stephen Covey and his wife both give an issue marks out of ten for importance to them. The one with the higher number makes the decision.

CHAPTER 11

Decision making as a heroic journey

Making a decision? Become a movie star! I find it very useful – and inspiring – to compare the journey of a decision, from the first awareness of the need for change to the ultimate realisation of goals, to the 'heroic journey' uncovered by Joseph Campbell and used as a model for many Hollywood movies.

Campbell analysed traditional stories from all round the world and found that they followed a similar pattern. This material was then used by Hollywood as a template for movie plots – *The Wizard of Oz* and *Star Wars* are classic examples. Here is a simplified version of the pattern that Campbell found.

The call

The story begins with a hero (the term is used to describe protagonists of either sex). They are usually in a state that is in some way unsatisfactory, for them and for others around them. They receive a *call* to get up and do something about this. This will mean going on a quest for a solution. Initially they often *refuse the call*, as it involves too much risk or simply inconvenient change; better to muddle along. However, things get worse, and some event changes the hero's mind so they *accept the call* after all.

In *The Wizard of Oz*, the song 'Somewhere Over the Rainbow' expresses Dorothy's true hearing of the call and her longing to get some real change in her life.

In terms of the Change House, the hero starts off in the Room of Denial, where they refuse the call, then move out of this room by accepting it.

For the decision maker, you hear the call the moment you initiate the four-stage process and step into the decision simulator. Incongruence can be a refusal of the call – but the hero's call won't go away, and nor does the need for important decisions. Accepting the call is entering on Stage 2 and committing to work towards the central decision.

Confusion to clarity

Accepting the call means that the hero has to leave their existing world and *cross a threshold* into a new one (for example, Alice falling down the rabbit hole). They cannot now turn back. In this new world, they will experience *confusion*. However, a view of how things are will soon become clear: the source of the trouble in the world they have left is a *demon*, and the demon is here in the new world and needs to be fought.

For the decision maker, crossing the threshold is similar to making the central decision and having lived with it for as long as needed. Up till then, you could always go back; from now on, the only way is forward.

It is useful to ask what exactly is the demon that you face. It's reasonable to expand the metaphor and say that you probably have more than one – Hollywood needs one big demon (played by Ralph Fiennes, Alan Rickman or, in an earlier era, Vincent Price or Christopher Lee); the decision maker may face a number of them. To go back to an example cited earlier, Jenny, in her decision to leave Paul, may well see her overbearing soon-to-be-ex as the demon, but she will have other demons, such as loneliness, to deal with once the decision is made.

Gathering help

The hero knows they have to fight the demon – and that they haven't a hope of doing so on their own. They have to find help. The help can often be a wise old man or woman with magical powers, who acts as a *mentor*. Other *helpers* are gathered or attach themselves to the voyager, too. The hero and their motley crew set off to do battle with the demon . . .

In the heroic model, the hero only starts gathering resources after they have crossed the threshold. Decision makers can start this earlier, as they prepare for the decision in Stage 2.

Decision making is in many ways a lonely business: when you are pacing up and down that room, on the brink of deciding, you know *how* lonely. But it is also an area where you can and should get as much help as possible – remember the advice on coaching and mentoring in Chapter 4. Our troubleshooting guide is one such source of help, of course.

The battle

The demon is finally confronted, fought and overcome. To make the story exciting, the good guys usually fare pretty badly at first. Then there is a turning point. Often the hero has a *transformational moment*; they learn something of immense value or undergo some personal change that at last enables them to turn things around and win. Often the demon turns out to be vulnerable and rather feeble once it has been rumbled, and sometimes it can even be co-opted as a helper for the hero.

Many decisions involve a *Big Scene* where someone has to be told you are leaving them, quitting a job, going to Australia for a year (or whatever). This can be equivalent to the big movie showdown.

The transformation of the decision maker is often more drawn out than the dramatic one beloved of Hollywood. But it is every bit as powerful. Making decisions changes people.

> making decisions
> changes people

The gradual 'shrinking' of the demon to something much more vulnerable can happen in Big Scenes. Going back to Jenny's story, when she actually went and confronted Paul – with her friend sitting in her car across the road in case anything went wrong – and told him she was leaving, he simply nodded his head and said that he had also felt things hadn't been right for a while, apologised for being so unpleasant lately and said he admired her courage for coming out with the truth.

The more general demons, such as the loneliness Jenny was afraid would follow her becoming single again, can also turn out to be harmless or even helpful. Jenny has found she rather likes being alone, for the moment anyway, and is using the extra time she has for herself to read lots of books she's been meaning to read for years.

The general message – don't fear demons, they often turn out to be much less threatening than you think – is constant.

brilliant tip

Often the thing we fear most about making a decision turns out not to be harmful to us at all.

The return home

The hero often has to steal from the demon some kind of magic *elixir* that will right the wrongs of the world they left behind, then take that back to that world. This journey can be lengthy and sometimes difficult, with various barriers to be crossed or with forces trying to get their hands on the elixir.

The long journey back is an excellent metaphor for the need to 'stick at it' with a big decision – the need to keep going to the gym, to keep the relationship fun, to keep the business going when economic conditions decline.

There are often moments of *celebration* on the journey home, too, and this should be part of your long-term implementation. Celebrate passing milestones – another kilogram lost, your fifth anniversary, the bank loan you needed to set up now paid off.

The elixir itself stands for all the rewards you will gain from having made and implemented your decision. It is a key theme of this book that decisions are almost

> decisions are almost always better than inaction

always better than inaction. You may not get the rewards you think, but you will get real benefits – these are the elixir that you take into the next phase of your life, to brighten it, and to become a better, fuller person to brighten the lives of others, too.

I like this metaphor of decision making as a heroic journey. Decision making can be tough. Allow yourself to think of yourself as a hero as you go through the most painful parts of your decision. It's not a piece of idle self-flattery; it's true.

Conclusion

I hope that this book has shown you that decision making is a skill that can be learnt and developed continuously – you never stop learning. I hope it has shown you that big decisions are complex processes that take place over time, and that those that are not – snap decisions – still involve skills that can be acquired and worked on. I hope I have shown you that decision making is a subtle art: one that involves flexibility, patience, self-knowledge, curiosity and courage. Above all, I hope I have shown you that decision making is a tool for continuing personal development in all areas of your life. It isn't just something done by leaders, or by the rest of us only on rare occasions.

Both outside us and within, there are forces that do not want our best selves to control our lives. Inside, there are old hurts and the old defences we put up to protect ourselves. There are old beliefs – about the world and about ourselves – that maybe once served us (or earlier generations) but which now hold us back. Outside, there are people with agendas: some who wish us well but who still want us to act out certain roles; and some who simply want to use our time, attention, money or votes to further their own ends.

We can decide to be free from these forces; free to contribute to the individuals we choose and to the world in general, in our own, unique way. We achieve this freedom by deciding to take it, and deciding when and how and in whose company we take it, and by deciding well, with all the skills we can muster. Such decision making, and the taking and best using of the freedom that comes with it, is the work of a lifetime.

I wish you good learning and well-deserved success with this adventure.

Further reading

Two books taught me a great deal about the neurology of decision making. They are A *General Theory of Love* by Thomas Lewis, Fari Amini and Richard Lannon (Vintage Books, 2001), and *The Decisive Moment* by Jonah Lehrer (Canongate Books, 2009). I recommend them both highly.

The research at Goldsmiths and the University of Houston quoted on page 6 was written up in the *Economist* magazine of 16 April 2009. If you want the original academic reference, it is in the *Journal of Cognitive Neuroscience*, July 2009.

A book that helped me understand the importance of values in decision making is *What Matters Most* by Hyrum Smith (Simon & Schuster, 2001). I also find reading literature helpful here. Try *Atlas Shrugged* by Ayn Rand (Penguin Classics, 2007): her philosophy may be a bit extreme, but I found it a breath – or rather a blast – of fresh air.

Obviously, I recommend my own previous book, *Think Like an Entrepreneur* (co-authored with Chris West, Prentice Hall, 2008). This isn't just to boost sales – the book contains much material on how entrepreneurs learn to make good decisions, and also a number of NLP techniques to use when troubleshooting.

The Power of Now by Eckhart Tolle (Mobins, 2001) gave me a structure to understand how the unconscious works, and allowed me to live in, value and get the best from confusion.

The Conquest of Happiness by Bertrand Russell (Routledge Classics, 2006) provides excellent material on the context of lifestyle decisions.

Finally, if your decision making means you have do battle with some really fierce demons, go into that battle armed with *The Prince* by Niccolò Machiavelli (Penguin Classics, 2004).

nlp school
the art of change

Dear Reader

At NLP School I present inexpensive and regular public courses, from one-day training events through to full certified NLP Practitioner and Master Practitioner qualifications.

NLP training is an ideal way for people to raise their game in life skills, and also to begin a profound personal development journey. The longer courses are broken down into four or five monthly modules. This gives people the opportunity to practise and absorb the material in their day-to-day life. Over this time, a supportive and friendly culture develops that can be as beneficial as the training itself: delegates become part of a group of people from all walks of life, sharing the desire to make key decisions for positive change. Often close and lasting friendships are formed.

The courses are a rich, effective and enjoyable learning experience. You'll come away with insights and tools you can apply both at work and in the rest of your life – from negotiation, entrepreneurship and leadership, through to self-awareness, cognitive skills, improved relationships, health and inner peace.

All the ideas in this book are taught on our NLP training programmes.

I hope to meet you on one of my courses.

Warm regards

Robbie Steinhouse

To join an NLP training course or arrange in-house training, visit www.nlpschool.com, e-mail info@nlpschool.com or call +44 (0) 207 428 7915.

Index